ON RIGG COLLE E

PENr

A *Handbook*
of Techniques for
FORMATIVE
EVALUATION

JUDITH GEORGE   JOHN COWAN

A *Handbook*
of Techniques for
FORMATIVE
EVALUATION

MAPPING *the student's learning experience*

KOGAN
PAGE

First published 1999

Apart from any fair dealing for the purposes of research or private study, or criticism or review, as permitted under the Copyright, Designs and Patents Act 1988, this publication may only be reproduced, stored or transmitted, in any form or by any means, with the prior permission in writing of the publishers, or in the case of reprographic reproduction in accordance with the terms and licences issued by the CLA. Enquiries concerning reproduction outside these terms should be sent to the publishers at the undermentioned addresses:

Kogan Page Limited
120 Pentonville Road
London
N1 9JN
UK

Stylus Publishing Inc.
22883 Quicksilver Drive
Sterling
VA 20166-2012
USA

British Library Cataloguing in Publication Data

A CIP record for this book is available from the British Library.

ISBN 0 7494 3063 X

Typeset by Kogan Page Limited
Printed and bound by Clays Ltd, St Ives plc

CONTENTS

INTRODUCTION

WHY SHOULD YOU BOTHER WITH FORMATIVE EVALUATION?

We begin by explaining what we mean by the two critical words in this opening question; and as we do so, we will add another associated word into the bargain.

We take evaluation to be the process in which comparisons are made between aspirations, or targets or ideals, and reality; consequently a judgement emerges as a result. So it is evaluation, in accordance with our definition, when an examiner assesses a student in an examination or an assignment. It is also evaluation when a funding council compares a department with a set of criteria which describe the council's expectations of well-run departments, and as a result of that comparison reaches and publishes its judgement of the department. It is evaluation when an employee is appraised against the firm's norms, and receives a judgemental review report. Assessment and appraisal are thus simply particular types of evaluation, as are formative and summative evaluations.

> When the cook tastes the soup, it is formative evaluation; when the dinner guest tastes the soup, it is summative evaluation.[1]

We describe evaluation as *formative* when the intention is to identify scope and potential for improvement. An assignment is formatively assessed when the comments that the teacher makes to the student are intended to bring about improvement in the next submitted work. An appraisal is formative when the outcome is a list of suggestions and decisions for action, and for development.

In contrast, we will describe some evaluations as *summative* – these being judgements when the conclusion which is reached is, at least for the immediate future, the basis of one or more decisions which stem from that judgement – whether it is of the competence of a person or a department or an institution. It is a summative evaluation when an examiner judges a candidate fit to be issued with a driving licence. It is a summative evaluation when a student is awarded an Upper Second after the finals have led to that judgement. It is a summative evaluation when a candidate is judged worthy of promotion to senior lecturer, or to a chair.

Having established how we will use these words, we should without further delay proceed to the question with which we began: why, then, should we, as university teachers, bother with formative evaluation?

The justification for suggesting that today's university teachers give serious attention to the need for, and the practice of, formative evaluation, lies in four aspects of academic life nowadays:

1. Our society is one in which accountability is more and more demanded of professionals. Interestingly, however, in higher education (at least in the UK) this accountability starts with a self-evaluation by an individual teacher (or an academic department), rather than with an external judgement. It is to the advantage of academics to retain that involvement in the evaluation of their activity, and to ensure continuing respect for their evaluations. They are the more likely to do so if they engage in the process rigorously and from a basis of sound and objective self-criticism.

2. Our culture nowadays is coming to regard the habit of self-critical reflection that Schön has made familiar,[2] as part of the nature of professional behaviour. This moves the practitioner beyond Kolb's cycle, which concentrates on the *development* of abilities,[3] and where the question asked is 'how do I do it?'. The movement is towards a self-*judgement* couched in terms of 'how well do I do it?' – which must, of course, be prefaced by the previous analytical question.

3. The introduction of a system of accreditation for teachers in higher education (at least in the UK) formalizes this self-evaluative reflection within the process of portfolio building which forms at least part of the assessment. The habit of formative evaluation provides the candidate with both the evidence and the process to proceed to this stage of formal recognition.

4. In the past two decades or so, the context of learning and teaching has seen great advances in our understanding of how students learn. At the same time tremendous developments have occurred in the harnessing of new technologies to support and progress learning.[4] Furthermore, the expectations and demands of any system of education and of the educators within it have been given a radically changed orientation. The introduction of learning outcomes such as the development of key skills, an increasingly critical awareness of the processes of learning and consequent ability to learn how to learn, and the emphasis on fitness for employment once students obtain a degree have changed the nature of higher education. In

addition, the students themselves come from increasingly diverse social and economic backgrounds, with government pressure to make further and higher education yet more accessible to all sectors of the population. The changes occasioned by all of these factors have been planned and implemented in good faith; but they require to be evaluated iteratively, so that we can be assured of their effectiveness, and know rather than hope that their full potential has been realized. That iterative review and consequent progression should thus be informed by sound formative evaluation.

Past practice in curriculum development has relied on a form of self-review which has been moderately useful and was certainly well intentioned. However, it lacked the rigour and objectivity which are now expected of university teaching, and which have been found to be possible and beneficial. On occasions, many of us may have observed a colleague teaching, or have invited them to observe us. The purpose of this visitation was not to enable the observed teacher to pass a test or prove what good tutors we were, but simply to provide feedback from a peer about usual practice, which both parties could subsequently discuss and analyse. We – or most of us – are also in the habit of mulling over on our own how a class went or how effective that particular design of laboratory work proved to be. We, the writers, would call this form of unstructured, informal self-evaluation 'self-review', to distinguish it from the more rigorous forms of self-evaluation. The basis for this distinction lies in the informality and lack of rigour in the construction of the judgement, and the possible lack of quality in the evidence on which the judgement is based. For casual or informal self-reviews seldom systematically search out data relevant to identified queries, or come to a supported and well-founded judgement on the basis of that data.

The habit of reflective rumination[5] on teaching practice is valuable, and is not to be discouraged or disparaged. But in the context of the factors outlined above, we, as teachers, need to go beyond reflection upon *teaching*, and have to put to good use as much insight into and knowledge of our students' *learning experience* as we can obtain. For that reason we should try to work from valid data on which we can soundly and rigorously base our self-judgements and the outcomes which stem from them. On occasion, this evaluation may occur for summative purposes – such as in teaching quality assessment, or the formal review that an institution requires at the end of a presentation of a course or module. More often, to meet the other requirements listed above, we need to evaluate for formative purposes. From valid, illuminating and constructive insights gained in the midst of our supporting and teaching of students, we can identify where there is scope and need for improvement in the effectiveness with which we are meeting their needs and carrying out our purposes. The teacher who aspires to enhance quality thus needs access to a range of methods of enquiry that will provide suitable data upon which to base soundly such formative judgements of effectiveness.

This handbook, therefore, sets out to offer readers a range of techniques that a teacher without special training or assistance can use to inform formative evaluations, from the very midst of the action of everyday teaching and learning. We adopt a minimalist approach, in that virtually every technique we suggest is capable of being built easily and unobtrusively into the design of a tutorial or lecture. This avoids burdening the teacher with an extra time commitment, additional paperwork and so on. There are admittedly one or two exceptions in our collected assortment of methods – such as the process of interpersonal process recall[6] which readers may yet have to encounter – which are somewhat complex and demanding; but nevertheless we have included them with an accompanying caveat, because in our experience they are well worth while using occasionally.

We suggest that the variety and range of techniques which we present in this book is necessary in order that you can have access to an appropriate approach, whatever the design of the teaching and learning session and whatever the angle of enquiry you have in mind. For different techniques ask different questions about the learning – they may focus on the coverage, or the achievement of cognitive outcomes, the quality of group interaction and so on; and they will furnish you with different types of data upon which to base your self-evaluations. So, whatever the questions you wish to ask of the teaching and learning for which you are responsible, we hope you will find an appropriate suggestion within this book. We have cross-referenced techniques throughout the text, in the hope that you will not (only) read this book from cover to cover, but dip into it as a resource whenever you are thinking about this subject.

The methods we describe for you are all ones which we, or colleagues of ours, have used successfully in normal teaching and learning situations, and which we can thus vouch for as practicable and useful. Our account of the techniques themselves is given succinctly in the main body of the text, where we aim to set them in context, describe how they are carried out, explore their applications, and discuss how they contribute to the dialogue and relationship between teacher and student. In the main, we suggest methods in terms of a conventional teaching setting, and only rarely in the context of flexible, open or distance learning. To describe the variants on the themes for such situations would have been lengthy and cumbersome. We have accordingly decided to leave it to our readers' ingenuity to translate these techniques, as we ourselves have often done, into practicable variants for the great range of different learning and teaching environments.

We begin in Chapter 1 by setting formative evaluation firmly in the context of systematic curriculum development, since we believe strongly that it should be an integral part of any course or module development. We then go on to suggest how you should choose a particular method which will be relevant and productive for your particular purpose in investigating your students' learning.

We conclude the book with a brief Appendix, in which we give stage-by-stage instructions for some of the most useful and common methods where these involve the assistance of a colleague. These are presented in a form which you could photocopy, either for your own use, or for the use of a colleague you have co-opted to act as an enquirer (on your behalf) into your students' learning.

We would hesitate to claim that our handbook provides an exhaustive account of all possibilities, given the wide experience and imaginative expertise in this field. However, we hope that at least it provides a solid core of familiar and useful methods. Further, the taxonomy of methods and styles of evaluation is not a precise science. Readers may well find under our titles the description of a method that they know by another name.[7]

Notes

1. Quote with thanks to the *Evaluation Cookbook* (1998), ed J Harvey, Learning Technology Dissemination Initiative, Institute for Computer Based Learning, Heriot-Watt University, Edinburgh.
2. Schön, D (1984) *The Reflective Practitioner*, Basic Books, New York.
3. Kolb, D (1984) *Experiential Learning*, Prentice Hall, New York.
4. Laurillard, D (1993) *Rethinking University Teaching*, Routledge, London.
5. See, for example, Hewitt, P *et al* (1997) *How Do I Know I Am Doing a Good Job?*, Open Teaching Toolkit, Regional Academic Service, Open University, Milton Keynes.
6. For this methodology, see Method 4.2, page 123.
7. As far back as 1979, Williams listed 22 different titles which users claimed to describe a distinctive style of evaluation, and there have no doubt been many more added in the 20 intervening years. See Williams, N (ed) (1979) *An Introduction to Evaluation*, London Schools Council.

CHAPTER 1

APPROACHING CURRICULUM DEVELOPMENT SYSTEMATICALLY

WHERE DOES FORMATIVE EVALUATION FIT IN?

Most texts on curriculum development assume a linear model with a feedback loop (see Figure 1.1). Their linear process describes, in varying terms but with fairly constant features, the chronological sequence in which:

- aims and outcomes are determined;
- teaching methods and arrangements are chosen;
- teaching plans are prepared;
- teaching is delivered;
- students learn;
- teachers assess students;
- feedback is obtained from students (and perhaps others);
- the course is evaluated (usually by those who prepared and presented it);
- revisions are determined;
- the cycle begins again.

We have some difficulties with that sequence because:

- it assumes that aims and outcomes are only considered, and reviewed, once per cycle or iteration;
- it concentrates on teaching rather than learning;
- it presents learning as a consequence of teaching, rather than teaching as one, but not the only, input to learning;
- it obscures the relationships between the elements of process.

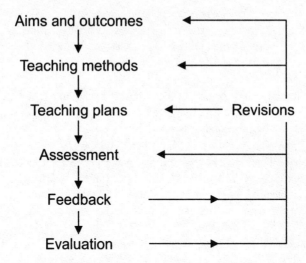

Figure 1.1 *Traditional curriculum development*

We, therefore, prefer to relate our thinking to the logical, rather than chrono-logical, model advanced by Cowan and Harding.[1] In this model, *aims* (which we are using as a portmanteau expression for 'aims, outcomes and/or objec-tives') are set at the centre (see Figure 1.2). The learning outcomes that we hope our learners will achieve are thus assumed, through the radial and mainly outward arrows, to influence and be influenced by all that occurs in the prepa-ration and presentation of the curriculum.

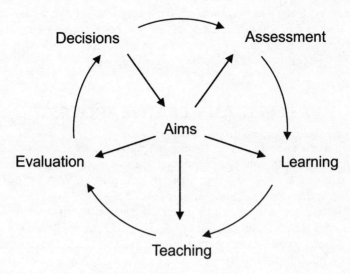

Figure 1.2 *A logical model for curriculum development*

The first element on the perimeter is then *assessment*, which is known from research to be the most powerful influence on student learning, well ahead of the declared syllabus or the published learning outcomes.[2] Hence this, logically, is the first circumferential arrow in Figure 1.2.

Learning will then be a response on the part of the student to the perceived messages from both the declared aims and outcomes, and the assessment – all of which, hopefully, will be giving the same messages.

Teaching, we believe, should then be designed to meet the needs of learners who are striving to meet the objectives inherent in the assessment, and critical to the aims. Learning styles, strategies and needs thus influence teaching, or should do so, through our next circumferential arrow.

We take *evaluation*, as we have explained, to be an objective process in which data about all that has gone before is collected, collated and analysed to produce information or judgements.

Subsequently *decisions* for action, including changes in aims, are made on the basis of the evaluation, and in terms of the course aims or goals. Such decisions will not usually be made by those who undertook the evaluation, and will preferably always involve the responsible teachers.

When the evaluation primarily leads, as we would hope it often does, from one iteration to the next, it is essentially formative. Hence it is formative evaluation which is the bridge between data collection and development. On the relatively rare occasions when purely summative evaluation is called for, a judgement of quality as an end product is desired, and there is no intention to move on to a further developmental iteration. Summative evaluation, therefore, is peripheral to the process of curriculum development.

WHY IS IT AN ITERATIVE PROCESS?

Iteration is at the heart of successful curriculum development; because, for each cycle to benefit from the experience of its predecessor, there must be a constructive link forward and into the next development. We need not apologize that this is so, for most good design – in any discipline – is iterative. When we teach something for the first time, even if it is only the first time for us, we prepare as thoughtfully as we can; but there will be some challenges that we underestimate, some factors that we do not anticipate, and some possibilities that we do not fully utilize. After our first presentation of this particular course or activity, we still expect to discover that improvement may be possible. And, if we care about our students and our teaching, we plan for such change – so that the second iteration will be an improvement on the first. We should, therefore, always be on the lookout for the information on which a well-grounded judgement for improvement will be based: for 'students are reluctant to condemn, and rate few teachers poorer than average'.[3] And so we need to seek such information rigorously.

Sadly, there are many educational decisions even today which are made for reasons that are unsound. They may stem from a desire to teach in a certain way, from a memory of teaching that proved effective for the teacher many years ago, or from habit or educational folk wisdom, or even from ignorance. Such decisions are ill-founded, even if they happen to lead to improvement. They do not build systematically and purposefully on the experience of a previous iteration. That is why we criticize them as unsystematic, and argue for the need to build instead upon a well-informed and accurate perception of the experience of the previous iteration – in order to improve the next one. Such a process gives the teaching of a subject the same rigour and sound basis as its content. This plea applies both at the micro-level – to the shaping of the introductory tutorial which you always give for new students, for example, or even the approach you take to teaching a particular concept or formula; and also at the macro-level – in the design and implementation of an entirely new course or module.

Arranging for formative evaluation is the means by which you can build into your present plans the possibility of an eventual refinement of what you are doing at present. It entails building in the opportunity to find out, as you go along, how things are for your current learners. It should be the means by which you find out whether what you planned is matched by what is actually happening for your students. It is the source of the data on which you will base your judgements about improvements and fine-tuning to be made. It is also the means by which, on a regular basis and within a familiar context, you check on how well you are doing as a teacher; *is* your students' experience actually what you hoped and intended? The habit of evaluative enquiry, over time, will help you to build up a well-founded professional expertise, so that, because of the rigorous way in which you have tested out and checked what you do, you can be more accurately informed about what works and what doesn't. Hence you will be building up a repertoire of teaching approaches and techniques which, you can be confident, will work well for your students. Such a basis for practice moves good 'amateur' work, derived often from no more than the accumulated, but perhaps unverified, experience of enthusiastic but unsystematic teachers, into the realm of true professionalism.

In addition to the findings of your formative evaluations, there will be other items of information from the wider context of the student learning environment. These can helpfully inform your process of development, but are incidental to your direct contact with and support of students. It is worth being aware of them and considering their potential use, in order to build review of them into your processes, if relevant. This data perhaps calls for some time and trouble to dig it out and analyse it, and might cover:

- entry qualifications;
- patterns of take-up for options;
- pass, fail, transfer and drop-out rates;
- rates of progression towards merits and honours;
- patterns of distribution of marks;
- first degree destinations;
- attendance patterns, levels of attentiveness and readiness to commit;
- patterns of choice in essays, projects and exam questions;
- comparisons with other programmes and their evaluations.

We note here the value of such collections of data,[4] especially since they are becoming increasingly easy to access and analyse, as institutional records are computerized. And we would put in a plea that, as institutional and information technology (IT) change is planned, it is important to consider making such data more easily available to teachers, as it is directly relevant to their understanding of their students.

WHAT APPROACHES TO EVALUATION ARE THERE?

Researchers have identified three main approaches to educational evaluation. Firstly, and commonly, it is possible to concentrate on producing quantitative records of such items as teachers' efficiency and effectiveness, and learners' progress. For example, testing learners before and after a lesson can be a means of measuring the learning that the test identifies as occurring, or not occurring, during the lesson. Drop-out rates and attendance records may say something about motivation, and students' perceptions of teachers. These *behaviourist* or *quantitative* approaches, which concentrate on behaviour that can be measured, and on outcomes that have or have not been achieved, feature useful information.[5] But you should be aware that they do not cover interpersonal processes or any unintentional outcomes of the teaching and learning situation, which may or may not also prove valuable input to an evaluation.

An option is to attempt to identify all the effects of the course provision, and relate these to the rationally justifiable needs of the learners. Such an approach, usually termed 'goal-free', will obviously depend considerably on open-ended questionnaires, unstructured interviews, record keeping, and on the rationality and objectivity of teachers, learners and especially of evaluators.[6] We suggest that this is more readily obtainable, and more feasibly resourced, in full (and summative) educational evaluation, than in the type of enquiry which you will have in mind, as a busy teacher.

Finally, there is a family of approaches variously termed 'illuminative' or 'transactional' or 'qualitative'.[7] These attempt to identify a broad view of a range of expectations and processes, and of ways in which the programme is seen and judged, including its unexpected outcomes. This is the grouping to which we relate most of the approaches in this handbook, especially if you take our advice to combine several methods of enquiry to obtain a range of perspectives on your teaching and your students' learning. It will not concern you that the findings of such evaluations do not generalize well, for you only wish to focus on your own teaching and your students' learning. But you should be aware nonetheless that qualitative approaches run the risk, in unskilled hands, of subjectivity and relativism. And, in any case, you may wish to triangulate qualitative data of a significant nature with a larger sample of students to establish its quantitative validity.

We should declare here our own preference for a version of what is termed 'illuminative evaluation'. This follows a process of progressive focusing in which the evaluator on behalf of the teacher(s):

- does not set out with a predetermined purpose to verify or dispute a thesis;
- tries to observe without being influenced by preconceptions and assumptions;
- thus attempts to observe, consider and study *all* outcomes;
- nevertheless pays particular attention to any emerging features that appear to warrant such attention;
- reports objectively and descriptively, without judgement – implied or explicit.

Notice, however, that this approach demands a separate evaluator, and additional resources. We can on occasions transfer some of the open-endedness of illuminative evaluation into our own modest formative evaluations. However, on the whole, these must necessarily be focused by our immediate needs as teachers and as planners of development.

WHAT KIND OF INFORMATION DO YOU NEED FROM FORMATIVE EVALUATION?

We advise you to begin by working out the place of formative evaluation within the *macro*-level of what you do. That means thinking first of enquiries which will be made within the wide canvas of an enquiry about a particular course or module design, or a curriculum innovation. However, techniques of formative evaluation are equally relevant and indispensable at the *micro*-level for an enquiry into a particular tutorial or element of your teaching style. But we consider it of primary importance that you begin by building the time and opportunity for systematic evaluation into any and every curriculum development.

In that context, your focus as a teacher may be on any aspect of what is happening in the current iteration which can assist you to bring about improvement next time. Naturally, your first concerns will be the nature of the actual learning outcomes, and of the learning experience. You may want to know, for example, if your carefully designed computer-assisted learning (CAL) materials *did* lead to high post-test scores, or if the students do not manage to analyse as you have taught them, or if your examination does not test learning according to the learning outcomes you have set as your aims. Equally it will be helpful if an illuminative evaluation reveals the minor features of the CAL programme which have irritated or frustrated learners, and could be readily improved; or if it transpires that, while your tutorials concentrated on cognitive needs decided by you, the needs which mattered most to your students were affective. If you are to engage in formative evaluation, for the most part you will be your own evaluator. And the detachment that an illuminative evaluator could bring to the process is something you should aspire to emulate, even if you have to undertake the evaluative tasks yourself.

Perhaps it will help to summarize here the range of information that you as a teacher should hope to obtain, so that your development into the next iteration can be well grounded and thorough. Following our model of curriculum development, the questions for which you should have informed answers when you are at the stage of deciding how to refine and develop your curriculum might include:

1. Does the assessment effectively test achievement of the aims and outcomes?
2. Does the assessment convey an accurate message to the learners about what they have to learn, and the standard that they should reach?
3. Are the learning outcomes realistic and appropriate?
4. Are the learning activities in the plan appropriate to the aims and learning outcomes that have been adopted?
5. Does the teaching activity support learning of the type and direction specified?
6. Have adequate arrangements been made to ingather information about all these matters, and to analyse the outcomes for presentation in a form that will be helpful to those responsible for the next development?

It is our frank opinion that few teachers and course teams in current practice have sufficient information to enable them to formulate their own answers to these questions. Equally, it is our view that current practice is sadly deficient in methods that are capable of being used by serving teachers to obtain such data. Rectifying that omission or relative neglect will make our curriculum developments more systematic – and more effective.

WHAT, THEN, SHOULD YOUR FORMATIVE EVALUATION COVER?

The focus of formative evaluation, the methods used to obtain the relevant data, and the form of data, can vary greatly. Referring to the previous list, for example:

- *The match of assessment to aims/learning outcomes* – calls for careful analysis of the demands of the assessment *in toto*, and in particular of the treatment of threshold performances which lead to pass marks or decisions.
- *The message conveyed to learners by the assessment scheme* – must include the format through which it is presented. This is something that can probably only be ascertained through careful interviewing of students, or perhaps in protocol studies,[8] as learners encounter assessment demands.
- *The appropriateness of the demands of the learning outcomes, as defined* – should be validated by checking them against the benchmarks of that particular academic field, against the coherence of the outcomes of this module with those of the entire learning programme of the students in this discipline, against the demands of a professional body (where relevant), and against the experience of graduates in their careers after graduation, and of their employers who may have had unfulfilled expectations.
- *The relationship between the chosen learning situations and the aims/outcomes in the plan* – can partly be judged on a detached pedagogical basis, and partly on the extent to which they, without support or remedial teaching, assist the learners to achieve the desired outcomes.
- *The effectiveness of the teachers and of the teaching* in supporting the intended learning – can best be judged by detailed studies of process and of immediate outcomes.
- *The adequacy of the evaluation methods and practice* – are a matter for detached and expert judgement; but, in addition, the teachers will naturally judge them by the usefulness and authority of the findings which emerge, to be input into the process of further development.

HOW WILL YOU DEAL WITH THE OUTCOMES, AND PLAN ACTION?

The analysis of findings,[9] and the use of these analyses to inform and guide decisions, is not something which you must do on your own, or without reference to what others have done before you. It is deceptively easy to be strongly influenced by your first impressions of evaluative data, especially if you have no systematic approach to identifying what feedback does, and does not, reveal. It is sensible to involve colleagues to help you to make sense of findings and decide implications and priorities for action.

Be especially wary of your reactions to what is commonly described as 'feedback', whether it is derived from questionnaires or staff–student focus groups or committees. It is all too easy to feel, or worse still, to display, anger or disappointment when you hear or read a negative message. Equally, if the programme came out of the evaluation reasonably well, or if only a few points were shown to be unsatisfactory, it is tempting to settle placidly for the decision that no action is needed. The involvement of a helpful colleague can ensure that you do not summarize weaknesses without being equally ready to summarize strengths, or that you do not fail to follow up issues whose presence is clear, but whose detail is not.

It is also important to think from the outset about how you may best get the most out of the data which your chosen form or forms of evaluation can produce. In many cases, the product will be self-evident; concept maps drawn at the end of an activity[10] for example, should give you a description of what students are aware of having learnt or developed during that activity. Thus you have information simply about learning outcomes.

In other cases, the data can be rich – and complex. This would be the case in the findings that may result from an 'unpacking' of a student's total experience. These may cover needs and difficulties in learning *during* the activity; feelings; mismatches between the plan for the activity and the preferences of the learners; and even reasoned suggestions for improvement. In such a case, you may wish to work from a detailed analysis, with careful notes on the points of significance to you.

Before we move on to suggested methods of evaluation, we wish to highlight the need to be thinking not only about what you want or need to know to inform the systematic process of curriculum development, but also about how you will interpret what is reported to you in the evaluation, whoever conducts it.

How you set out the findings for analysis and decision-making may be significant. You may find it useful to devise a visual format for the feedback, if you prefer visual, rather than verbal, information. With qualitative data, standard forms such as pie or bar charts are an obvious choice. But you may find it helpful to devise a more personal format that makes sense to you. For example, one of us has an inclination to count and note predominant groupings in little tables, in which perhaps the rows are for different parts of the curriculum, and the columns are headed with types of feedback message. This format of summary can make it quickly possible to see clearly, for example, that it is in certain parts of the curriculum that evaluators report a high frequency of questions in class, in others a popular choice of one particular assignment topic, and in yet a third, heavy use of texts in the library.

In another and rather different example, a colleague draws a circle, and marks the circumference with evenly distanced points, which he labels with significant criteria. Drawing a line from the centre to each point on the circumference, he rates along the line for each factor, on a scale of 1 (in the centre) to 10, where he thinks the feedback places him. He then interconnects the marks on each line, thus giving himself a pattern of quantitative judgement not only for each factor, but also for the interconnections between the factors.

Whatever approach you decide upon, do ensure that your actions and reactions are based on objective data and findings, and do not merely rely on 'gut reactions'.

DON'T NEGLECT THE STUDENTS!

It will be clear from much of what we write about particular methods of formative evaluation that we see this activity as something in which, at best, teachers and learners share and have differing contributions to make. For that reason it is important to ensure that student involvement continues after the data has been assembled and analysed.

That seems obvious. Yet we often encounter situations in which students provide feedback, but are not told what their feedback, in aggregate, said – or what action the teachers propose to take as a result. There should be no reluctance to make findings known to those who contributed to them even if there can be difficulties in making raw results public, without first obtaining everyone's permission. It is the relevant way of showing how you value this activity, and your students' part in it; it is also a way of putting their learning experience on the agenda for you and them. Our experience has often been that the process of seeking formative data has in itself initiated and opened up a deep dialogue about learning between the students and teacher, which has strengthened their relationship and mutual understanding, and has enriched the total process because of the extra dimension which joint discussion produces.

At the same time, beware of giving unbalanced weight to student feedback. It is all too easy for a concerned teacher to blame the teaching for low ratings – without also considering the possibility that the subject is demanding, the resources poor, the staff or students badly briefed, or that the prerequisites or coursework have been insufficiently covered by the students, who may have spent too much time in the pub, or may have taken on part-time employment to bolster their finances.

And, finally, you must be honest with the students when they have criticized something which cannot be changed or over which you have no control – if possible, anticipating such frustration by declaring the constraints beforehand.

THE RELATIONSHIP BETWEEN FORMATIVE AND SUMMATIVE EVALUATIONS

It would be unfortunate if we conveyed the impression that we see the distinction between formative and summative evaluations as a dichotomous one – based on purposes that vary from improvement to appraisal. For we, ourselves, practise evaluations in a style which links formative and summative forms, and which in some ways moves somewhat steadily from an emphasis on the former to an emphasis on the latter.

Perhaps it will be simplest to explain this in terms of an example. One of us has recently been partly responsible for a development that has had several unusual features:

- The learning outcomes relate to personal development and the ability to manage that.
- The entire module is student-directed.
- The module is of 10 weeks duration.
- The students concerned are general studies students who are not noteworthy for their academic achievements to date.
- The module calls for reflective journalling by the students.
- These journals are submitted and commented upon electronically.
- There is a strong emphasis on self-assessment.
- Class meetings are interactive, and do not involve much in the way of input from the teachers.

Clearly the module is somewhat innovative, at least for the teachers concerned. The evaluative sequence has thus taken a developmental emphasis, and will continue to do so.

In year 1 (now completed) there was a clear demand to supply for the benefit of the review process a summative evaluation which would reassure the faculty that this tentative development was delivering as promised. Nevertheless, the emphasis for those teaching the module was on formative evaluation – which would help them to discover aspects of the provision that required or would benefit from attention. The tasks and activities in some cases failed to realize what was expected of them; they had to be revised. The assessment proved over-, and in some cases under-, demanding for the students; that also had to be rethought. The overall evaluation was positive; and so the summative demand was satisfied; but the formative message was that there were major aspects of the scheme that could well be improved. In the first year it was offered, formative evaluation was dominant, focusing on major features, and yet summative evaluation was also demanded by a society unwilling to await development and refinement before reaching a judgement.

In the second year of presentation, the module progressed fairly satisfactorily. It was a simple matter to satisfy the demands of faculty for a reassuring summative evaluation. However, for those teaching the module, there were messages emerging from yet another searching formative evaluation, which suggested refinements of merit.

So the development proceeds to year 3, wherein it will be necessary, in the view of those concerned, to prepare for a summative evaluation which will be meaningful to *them*, as opposed to external reviewers. The main emphasis in this evaluation, the innovators feel, should be the extent to which the innovation is addressing new aims, and achieving new outcomes. And so the first iteration of summative evaluation, if responding to that view, will be one which seeks to establish the full range of learning outcomes in the new provision – and not merely to test the module against the declared learning outcomes.

Finally, in yet another year, having established the full range of learning outcomes, it is hoped that the summative evaluation will establish the extent to which these outcomes, planned and unplanned, have been achieved. At the same time, the desire of the teachers to continually seek need for and means of improvement should imply that formative evaluation is not neglected.

We thus suggest that the distinction between formative and summative evaluation is best seen as a balance, which in the early stages of development will emphasize formative rather than summative evaluation; and which, in later stages, will dwell on the reverse balance. However, nonetheless, the evaluations in each iteration will entail some enquiries and analyses with both formative and summative intentions, albeit in differing proportions.

EDUCATIONAL ENQUIRIES – A CASE STUDY DESCRIBING MODES OF ENQUIRY

We hope that it may be helpful at this point to digress slightly from our main theme, and present a recent example of curriculum development as a brief case study to illustrate the respective roles of formative evaluation, action research, and other forms of educational enquiry. The example comes from the initial delivery in Perth and Inverness Colleges of the University of the Highlands and Islands Project's (UHIP) degree of BA (Social Science).

In one of the modules on this course, students wrote reflective learning journals each week, and submitted them for comment – and for marking. A tutor commented on the journals in what was intended to be a facilitative manner, with development of the abilities of analytical and evaluative reflection as a primary goal. This activity was decidedly new to the students, and even to most of the tutors. The course team judged it imperative to fine-tune their operation, without waiting for end-of-module evaluations. Therefore, once the students had had sufficient time to feel acclimatized to the new demand, they were invited to suggest to their tutors the type of comment that they now knew they would find most useful.

We regard this embryonic and highly individual form of 'stop/start/continue' activity[11] as *feedback* in that it reached the tutor almost immediately, and produced speedy results for the individuals who responded. Such obtaining and using *feedback* is an activity in which teachers choose an appropriate form of enquiry to obtain information which is as relevant and as comprehensive as possible. They then analyse the findings and respond to them in time for the students who provided the feedback to benefit from the changes made as a consequence.

Then, at the conclusion of the first semester, the UHIP tutors followed a practice that was begun in the bridging course. This course was provided for students with an HND who were entering Level 3 study of degree level work. On the final afternoon of what was a demanding and intense fortnight, the tutors had structured an activity to provide them with information about the students' experience and their learning. In this, they tabled several questions of importance to them, together with the opportunity for students to concentrate on their own choice of topics. The tutors suggested how information could be extracted and assembled in their absence, and how open-ended responses and judgements could be formulated. This was all an application of the development within the module of the ability to make and use judgements.

From the report that the students produced, the tutors learnt of the successes and some weaknesses in the bridging course. That information came too late to profit the current cohort – but certainly informed the revision, and consolidation, of the bridging module for the next cohort of HND students approaching level 3 studies as they neared the end of their HND studies in session 1998–99.

We regard this workshop activity as *formative evaluation,* understanding by that an enquiring activity in which the evaluators rigorously ingather information which informs the process of review and revision.[12] This evaluation will normally bridge between one iteration of delivery and the next, but may well occur in mid-module, and enhance what is done subsequently. Because of its rigour, and the widening angle of enquiry, it may also produce generic observations of more extensive interest.

Each learning journal, as we have described, was commented on by a tutor who attempted to follow a Rogerian approach.[13] This meant that the journal writers were to be treated with unconditional positive regard, and that the commentator conscientiously and consistently attempted to display empathy and congruence.

In these circumstances, the course team and the tutors directly concerned were conscious of developing a pedagogy for which they could find little precedent or advice in the literature. The tutors' style was strongly (but perhaps wrongly) influenced by the prior experiences of one of them with this type of learning activity.[14] It was, therefore, of great importance to the tutors to progress their practice, through awareness and scrutiny of those aspects of it which became established, or about which they had firm views. They tackled this self-imposed challenge in two ways.

First, they were determined to move as close to the student experience as possible; and so they each kept their own weekly reflective journal, dealing with *their* learning, in the broadest sense of that word, in *their* experience of the course that week. They worked to the same remit as they had given their students. And they commented on each other's journals in the same way as they commented on the students' journals.

Secondly, one of them (who had more research time) used Kelly's Repertory Grid[15] to identify the factors in journals which promoted comment, the frequency of the various types of prompts and the types of response made to each category of prompt. This data, once analysed, provided them with an informed basis for self-scrutiny and for joint consideration of their rationale for commenting on journal entries. We regard these enquiries and the analyses that followed from them as *action research*.

We take *action research*, in the context of education, to be the conducting of investigations of a researching nature which produce useful findings relevant only to the particular situation and people and subject studied, from which the findings were obtained.

During the spring term of 1999, the two tutors correlated their experiences and findings in the above and similar action research activities in UHI with those from a rather different situation in Heriot-Watt University. There, students of the Personal Development Planning module maintained electronic reflective journals, which were an integral part of the teaching and learning activities in the module. They were expected to follow the Kolbian style of analytical reflection.[16] The tutors also related all these findings to such reports as are available in the literature from those who have used and commented upon reflective learning journals, and who have published more than anecdotal accounts of that. We regard this as a movement into what we call *educational research*.

We take *educational research* to be an investigative activity that produces and justifies generalized conclusions and recommendations, which can validly be applied to other (similar) teaching and learning situations from those in which the original data were obtained.

The four categories we have attempted to establish appear to differ markedly – especially in purpose, but also in applicability; and in that sense they may seem to be distinct:

1. *Feedback* should lead to changes of immediate benefit to the learners from whom it is obtained; in contrast, formative evaluation usually leads to benefit for the following cohort of students.
2. *Formative evaluation* is explicitly and immediately directed towards development; in contrast, action research may well focus on a deeper appreciation of the nature of the learning and of the learning experience, with only long-term outcomes for the teaching and learning.
3. *Action research* is unashamedly restricted to particular subjects, teachers and situations; in contrast, full educational research should be generalizable.
4. *Educational research* pushes out the borders of what is known about education, and hence contributes to the enhancement of informed professional practice.

However, there is equally an argument to be made for the location of our four categories of enquiry on a continuum of development, with a grey area of overlap between stages, rather than any sharp discontinuity.

Action research studies yield findings that are likely to provide much information of use in formative evaluation; and the methodologies that are used or developed in such studies lend themselves to adaptation for routine use in formative evaluation. Similarly, the approaches that stand up to scrutiny for their suitability in evaluations are often well suited to everyday use in providing feedback. We cite as an example the development of the Dynamic List of Questions,[17] which entered life in an action research study of importance to a project developing computer-assisted learning materials in Mathematics Education. It was then used in the Open University (OU) in Scotland, for formative evaluation of a number of curricular developments.[18] And it has also become part of the lesson plan for many OU tutors, who use it to obtain routine feedback about learning needs, and about the learning needs which are outstanding when a tutorial session has come to an end.

Equally, action research can develop naturally into educational research of less particular relevance. Examples of this include the early pioneering developments in the influence of self-assessment on learning, which have eventually contributed to a developing field of educational research.[19]

If formative evaluation is the key to systematic curriculum development, then it is equally arguable that action research is the natural development for and from rigorous formative evaluation, with links back to evaluation and feedback, and on into full educational research. Moreover, the centrality of both to the professional development of teachers is demonstrated by the requirements of the Institute for Learning and Teaching; in future a teacher in higher education will be required to demonstrate continuing professional development by means of portfolio work built up from the data of both formative evaluation and action research.

The key issue is the rigour and objectivity of the enquiry, and of the analysis – two features which are not particularly common in routine approaches to feedback, for example, or even in methods of formative evaluation which do not have their roots in one type of research or another. Such a systematic and objective process under any one of these headings, followed through on an iterative pattern, makes a powerful contribution to curriculum development.

Notes

1. See Cowan, J and Harding, A G (1986) A logical model for curriculum development, *British Journal of Educational Technology*, 2 (17), pp 103–09.
2. See Snyder, B R (1971) *The Hidden Curriculum*, MIT Press, Cambridge, MA, who has been quoted by many others who have explored this influence on learning.
3. Page, C F (1974) *Student Evaluation of Teaching – The American experience*, Society for Research into Higher Education, London.
4. See also Calder, J (1994) *Programme Evaluation and Quality*, Kogan Page, London. She outlines many aspects of the developmental stage of a course or programme which are not strictly formative evaluation, but which contribute significantly to the quality of work; peer comment, for example, instructional design input, student advocacy, quality improvement workshops, developmental testing and piloting.
5. For example, Tyler, R W (1949) *Basic Principles of Curriculum and Instruction*, University of Chicago Press. Tyler was the originator of this approach.
6. For example, Scriven, M (1973) Goal free evaluation, in *School Evaluation: The politics and the process*, ed E R House, University of Berkeley, CA.
7. On the value of illuminative enquiry, see Parlett, M and Hamilton, D (1972) *Evaluation as illumination: a new approach to the study of innovatory programmes*, Occasional Paper 9, Centre for Research in Educational Sciences, University of Edinburgh.
8. See Method 3.5, page 119.
9. On this and other aspects of evaluation we have found a valuable and accessible resource in Robson, C (1993) *Real World Research: A resource for social scientists and practitioner-researchers*, Blackwell, Oxford. On analysis of findings, see pp 303–408. Another valuable resource is Tessmer, M (1993) *Planning and Conducting Formative Evaluations*, Kogan Page, London, which, unlike the present work, is primarily focused on teams conducting formative evaluation before a programme is finalized.
10. See Method 5.1, page 65.
11. See Method 6.9, page 90 for the description of this activity as a technique of formative evaluation.
12. The feedback of the previous example would become formative evaluation if taken across a full class group, analysed and reviewed as in Method 6.9, page 90.
13. That is, following the approach of Carl Rogers in which teaching is seen as a facilitation akin to counselling, with three main constituents – unconditional positive regard, empathy and congruence. See Rogers, C R (1967) *On Becoming a Person*, Constable, London.
14. See Cowan, J (1986) *Education for Capability in Engineering Education*, D.Eng thesis, Heriot-Watt University, Edinburgh.
15. See Method 4.1, page 121.
16. See Kolb, D A (1984) *Experiential Learning*, Prentice Hall, New York.
17. See Method 3.2, page 115.
18. See Cowan, J et al (1988) *Report on project to assess tools for formative evaluation*, Open University in Scotland, Edinburgh.
19. See, for example, Boyd, H R, Adeyemi-Bero, A and Blackhall, R F (1984) *Acquiring professional competence through learner-directed learning – an undergraduate*

perspective, Occasional Paper No 7, Royal Society of Arts, London; Cowan, J (1984) *Learning contract design: a lecturer's perspective*, Occasional Paper No 7, Royal Society of Arts, London; Boyd, H R and Cowan, J (1986) The case for self-assessment based on recent studies of student learning, *Assessment and Evaluation in Higher Education*, **10** (3), pp 225–35.

CHAPTER 2

CHOOSING A METHOD OF FORMATIVE EVALUATION – AND USING IT

WHAT DO YOU WANT TO KNOW?

The starting point for your choice is, of course, what you want to evaluate. You may have in mind a very broad area; for example, your students' learning experience in general on your course, or their reactions to your teaching style. On the other hand, your query may be a focused and specific one about the course, the learning environment or your support, the effectiveness of the overheads you used in a particular lecture, the perceived welcome of the introductory session, or the way in which you introduced a new and challenging concept.

A caveat: your choice of a focus could be a two-stage process

On occasion, you may not be able to decide immediately on the exact focus of your enquiry. For example, you might have learnt that the use of CAL drill packages has significantly enhanced learning in a similar course in another institution, and in your own course you judge that there is clear scope for improvement; or you could have seen evidence in examination performance that certain topics are less well grasped than others; or you may have had adverse feedback at a staff–student committee meeting on the tutorial provision. In the first example, you will be well advised to try another approach initially, and then carry out a comparative evaluation – once the new option has been debugged and is reasonably well established. In the last two examples, you will need more information about the status quo before planning changes, and so will probably want to investigate and iterate towards improvement, by using some method of formative evaluation within the existing provision.

In such situations, it is probably wise to identify and assess any presuppositions which you, or others, are making about the cause of the weakness you wish to minimize or eradicate. Indeed, your first step in any formative evaluation may well be akin to deciding, in the broadest terms, where to aim the telescope of enquiry. If examination performances in your part of a course imply weak learning, should your formative evaluation concentrate on the teaching, the support for student activity, the textbook, the style of examination question, the lack of preparation for examination in that format, or the conflicting demands and attractions of other options in the examination paper? Without further information, you cannot make a defensible choice of focus. A preliminary enquiry will help you to decide where to look more closely, and what data you need to acquire about that aspect of the teaching, learning and assessment. Your formative evaluation will thus be in two stages – first a broad frame enquiry, to determine where to aim a more focused study later; then the focused study.

There is another sound, but different, reason for undertaking an enquiry in two stages. Through no lack of competence or experience, you may need a preliminary run to fine-tune the method of enquiry itself before applying it to the range of subjects or situations from which you wish to obtain data. For example, a recent evaluation was prompted by complaints from students who maintained that the assistants who provided tutorial support did not explain clearly when they were asked for help. An initial set of interviews revealed the interesting outcome that only the poorer students in the class group reported difficulty in comprehending the explanations which they sought and were given; their assertion (understandably) was that the assistants couldn't explain to students what they had to do. Amplification of the answers to follow-up questions asked by the evaluators revealed that poorer students were dissatisfied with the responses from assistants when they (the students) were asking what to do, in the expectation that the assistants would, in effect, do the thinking for the students. In this case the two-stage evaluation process was necessary to permit refinement of the methodology, to concentrate on students' expectations of teaching and their interpretation of course aims.

Be prepared, then, for formative evaluation to take place in two stages, and to be more useful as a result.

THE PURPOSE SHOULD DETERMINE THE METHOD

Many departments and course teams, when asked about evaluation during teaching quality assessment or quality audit, will respond confidently that their university has a standard questionnaire which is used at the conclusion of every module. The inference is that the use of a questionnaire meets the need for formative evaluation and, indeed, for summative evaluation into the bargain. Yet that is demonstrably unsound reasoning, for a questionnaire, like any other method of formative evaluation, covers only part of the range of matters which merit regular reconsideration.

One of the writers introduced tape–slide tuition to his undergraduate course at a time when that approach was relatively new. His students warmly praised the method, and would have confirmed that verdict if given a questionnaire to evaluate their reactions. They asked for more of this type of teaching – because they had 'learnt so much from it, so easily'. He then asked them to take a simple 90/90 post-test to test their learning anonymously. The result should have been that 90 per cent of the students scored at least 90 per cent on the factual recall test. This was far from the case, to the students' frank surprise. The moral of this little tale is that learning should be evaluated by finding out what students have *actually* learnt, not by what they *think* they have learnt. Questionnaires can surely only elicit factual information of which students have direct knowledge, such as the number of hours of study they put in during a typical week. Otherwise questionnaires obtain opinions. (Questionnaires may even only elicit opinions about the number of hours devoted to study!) Note, however, that the post-test which ascertained learning from the tape–slide sequence did not determine student *reaction* to the innovation, which was also important. The determination of the purpose of enquiry should, then, be matched by the choice of an appropriate method of evaluation; and vice versa.

In broad terms, the purposes that we may have in deciding to undertake some formative evaluation could be categorized under at least four distinct headings. Some methods, such as post-testing or the analysis of students' work, can tell us where *learning* has, and has not, taken place. Others, such as observations, briefed or unbriefed, and the taking of protocols,[1] can tell us about the *learning experience,* rather than the learning outcomes. Yet other methods, such as interpersonal process recall,[2] concentrate on feelings and reactions during learning, that is, the *immediate reactions* to the learning experience. And a final group, as we are choosing to divide them, may inform us of the *values* which students place upon the learning or the learning experience, for whatever reasons – as revealed, for instance, by the writing of letters from students to their successors, in the next academic year.[3]

We, therefore, suggest to you that you should plan evaluation by choosing a method or methods appropriate to what you or your course team want to know rather than, as is often the case, choosing a method for no relevant reason, with the outcomes which follow in consequence, appropriately or otherwise.

THE POTENTIAL TO BRING ABOUT CHANGE IS AN IMPORTANT CONSIDERATION

A detailed study of the effects of modularization on assessment loading for students and staff, and on the assessed coverage of the syllabus, was conducted in a department whose institution was firmly committed to modularization, and unlikely to make any changes in that policy. The analysis of the findings, and the presentation of them, took place in fora where the real agenda was to question the desirability of the *fait accompli* of modularization, despite the futility of that discussion. In a second and somewhat similar department, a comparable evaluation accepted the inevitable and set out to discover the aspects of learning that were suffering, and those that were not the subject of any deleterious effects. The result of that truly formative evaluation was to devise revised teaching and learning strategies and assessment methods to cope to an improved extent with what were perceived and accepted as the *de facto* constraints.

There is no point in engaging in formative evaluation that would focus on the need for changes in the unchangeable. Conversely, if we are in the business of bringing about change, it can be sound strategy, and far from devious, to engage in formative evaluation which should generate findings which will directly *influence* decision-making, as well as *inform* it. We instance an evaluation which confirmed the effect on learning of frequent testing, in a limited allocation of time, thus encouraging shallow rather than deep approaches. That study informed the decision-makers, but did not actually lead to any institutional change. However, when the next evaluation of the same situation followed a different tactic and showed (and publicized) higher retention scores in the modules where testing was less frequent and time pressures less acute, the majority of the departmental staff chose to modify their assessment practice and policy. Choice of focus for evaluation can strengthen its impact or render the effort pointless.

MULTIPLE PERSPECTIVES CAN ENHANCE EVALUATION, AND ITS USEFULNESS

Consider the possibility and potential of a situation in which three approaches to evaluation were adopted – and were chosen to concentrate on rather different aspects of the curriculum. The tutor, for example, arranged for:

1. Dynamic lists of questions,[4] which offered a proven means of judging the planning of class sessions and judging their perceived effectiveness. (*Primary purpose: to determine the students' perception of the effectiveness of these sessions in dealing with their perceived and declared learning needs*);

2. Blind second marking, by the tutor and others, of the students' submitted work, to a carefully formulated and agreed marking schedule.[5] *(Primary purpose: to confirm the objectivity of marking, and identify any scope for improvement in it)*;
3. A closing activity in class, making it possible for students to formulate advice to the tutor for next year on a 'stop/start/continue' basis – listing what not to do again next year, what to introduce next year, and what to retain for its strength.[6] *(Primary purpose: to identify scope for improvements worthy of consideration, and ongoing strengths that should be retained in the provision)*.

Among the outcomes of the evaluation were the following interrelated findings or suggestions:

- From (1), it was clear that outstanding questions on the dynamic lists were often in the form 'What other points of view should I know about, and consider?'
- From (2), although it was not the immediate focus of enquiry, it emerged that sections of the students' work which often attracted low, and unreliable, marks by assessors (including the main assessor when there was repeat marking) were associated with the students not taking a balanced view, in which optional possibilities and interpretations were properly considered.
- From (3), students were advising the tutor to stop asking them what *they* (the students) thought, and to start telling them more about what authorities in the field had made of such questions (shades of Perry!).[7]

While (1) and (3) had conveyed something of the same message, the findings in (2) pointed to a woolliness in the criteria and marking schedule, and even in the tutor's own thinking about that aspect of the learning. All of this, *taken together,* pointed to the need for the tutor to:

- think through the criteria associated with critical thinking and balanced review;
- communicate these criteria and goals more clearly to students;
- proclaim the criteria explicitly in marking schedules and in formative marking;
- structure part of the tutorials around the development of the required ability, probably with some provision, for example, for reflection on the process.

Notice how the multiple perspectives of a combined trio of approaches led to a deeper and more sensitive identification of, and response to, the need for a particular development in the teaching and assessment combined.

BEWARE YOUR OWN ASSUMPTIONS

- Watch out, for example, for your possible reliance on students' 'letters'[8] or wash-up reports, or other evaluations, which concentrate on aspects of the course which *you* have already made clear to them are important to *you* – such as developing critical thinking, and the accessibility of the tutor. Make sure you also find out about other aspects of the course, such as understanding of key concepts, and the clarity of the pre-course documentation, which you have been less energetic in emphasizing or providing. Adopt the approach that Karl Popper would advocate: concentrate on what may have been neglected, or not considered.
- Watch out for evaluations that concentrate on what you think is worth evaluating (which is not quite the same as the previous point). Make some provision for some other (external) source of focus for evaluations. It can be one of the most important outcomes of questionnaires, for instance, to suggest questions that need to be pursued, and have not so far received attention.
- Watch out for evaluating against criteria which you have not made explicit, and so are not scrutinizing as a matter of course. We recall an instance where the implicit criteria set such a high store on dealing with *dis*advantage (of various forms) that fairness in the treatment offered to the *non*-disadvantaged was losing out. That was not apparent until the criteria were made explicit, and were applied across the board of both tutor and course performance.

In such cases, the best response, once an evaluative weakness is identified, is usually to widen and strengthen your strategy, rather than to discard it.

CONSIDER RESOURCING CAREFULLY – ESPECIALLY IN TERMS OF HUMAN RESOURCE

We make this point through a few disconnected examples:

1. One of us learnt more about his students' learning, and made more changes in his teaching, as a result of taking and analysing recorded protocols[9] than from any other method of formative evaluation. But the price was one that he was not prepared to go on paying. Transcribing protocols is a dreary and difficult business. The subjects do not speak in carefully prepared or considered sentences, they often exclaim or mutter, and the tone and volume change continually. Despite the powerful

usefulness of recorded and transcribed protocols, that writer abandoned them as a feasible option, and sought second-best options with similar but rather less rich results.

2. Questionnaires are useful, but questionnaire surveys often lead to low return rates, because the students are left to return the forms at their leisure, and many do not do so. The result is often a statistically unreliable sample, which comes from a minority with particular reasons for responding – perhaps to log complaints, perhaps to praise. Responding in the students' own time is often accepted for expediency, because response time (in human resource terms) is judged something that cannot be spared in class to issue forms, and have them completed and returned. That is an unfortunate decision, and can have misleading outcomes. We have seen strongly worded evaluations – and consequent decisions – in course records, where the returns came from less than 20 per cent of the class group!

3. Interpersonal process recall,[10] in our experience, is often genuinely (and not evasively) discarded because it is seen as labour-intensive. It calls for perhaps two hours' time from a colleague, and 30 minutes each from two students and the tutor, to lead to outcomes to test at a later date against class opinion – in perhaps 15 minutes of class time. *Yet you would only do all this just once a year, or every other year.* Subjective decision-making notes the durations of effort, but not the frequency, but should balance the weighting in time commitment against the richness of the data acquired by this method. It is important to be sound in the judging of the demands on human resource, in terms of time.

IS THE EVALUATION LIKELY TO CONVINCE THOSE WHO RECEIVE IT?

We begin our answer from our own personal experience. We frequently recall that our early experiences of interpersonal process recall were shattering revelations – of important aspects of our teaching, and of its influence and impact on our learners of which we had hitherto been unaware. Yet it has been our experience, when frankly recounting examples of this to our peers during staff development activities, that they are somewhat dubious about the importance to our students of the findings which we narrate, and that they cannot quite see the need for us to have reacted as we did. We did not, we add, encounter that reaction from the learners who were to profit from the revelations, and our constructive reactions to them. The judgement of relevance, or of the adequacy of rigour in the findings of evaluations, depends on who makes the judgement, and how they judge satisfaction.

Notice, though, that formative evaluation can often be at its most effective when it does no more than suggest neglected aspects of the process which merit remedial or developmental attention. Observations of student reaction and behaviour may reveal lack of understanding, or may note questions from learners who are desperately seeking clarification about the subject, or may record actions at variance with the teacher's declared intentions. They may not rigorously establish *what* is wrong; but they are more than adequate to prompt a review and revision of the teaching and learning situation by showing that all is not well.

Always remember, though, and perhaps be reassured by the view, that there is a great risk in the worship of quantification, and its apparent rigour. Someone (at least one) has maintained sensibly that the things which matter cannot be measured, and the things which can be measured don't really matter.

THE PROCESS

Before formative evaluation begins

Let's just mention an obvious preliminary step. It should almost go without saying that you need to agree with the students a clear definition of the remit for the evaluation, even if and when you yourself evaluate, and a clear understanding of the role of anyone who assists you in that. If you are obtaining, or making public even within the class, information that is normally private or confidential, you must obtain permission to do so.

Analysing the data[11]

The important points to be made under this heading stem from the need for you to do all that should be done to ensure objectivity, and to avoid skipping hurriedly and carelessly through an important stage in the process.

You should separate the assembling of the data from the analysing of it. In the analysis, beware of the temptation to merely summarize and present that summary in a businesslike way. Look for patterns, and for inconsistencies – and point them out once they are found.

When you move on to interpret the data, and decide how to respond, be explicit – to yourself, your students and perhaps a helpful peer – about the values against which your decisions are then made as well as the actions you will take.

Think tactically – in terms of probable acceptability

If you first give thought to the way in which the outcome you hope for is likely to be received, this may suggest ways in which you would use or present your findings. Let's briefly consider a range of possibilities under this heading. You may wish to:

- *Reinforce a need for change*: one of us taught in a department where all the staff were agreed that the teaching of mathematics in schools had deteriorated dreadfully, and that many first year students were incapable of handling basic trigonometry. He eventually reached, and tried to confirm, a counter-hypothesis that it might be the inability of his students to deal with diagrams containing redundant lines, rather than an inability to handle basic trigonometric computations, which required remedial attention. He devised a test to ascertain the grasp of both abilities. He confirmed that the weakness on which remedial tuition was focusing was not present, while the suspected weakness was clearly present. The effort in remedial teaching then changed significantly, as a consequence of that finding – as did its effectiveness.

What was required here from formative evaluation was confirmation or otherwise of a view already formed, but not proven.

- *Amplify a suspicion*: we recall several situations in which we have suspected a need for change, and have wished formative evaluation to confirm this belief, and (in that case) to suggest means of achieving development. For example, observations of student behaviour during certain formal examinations, coupled with analysis of the marks scored for first, second, third and so on questions attempted, led one of us to suspect that students probably did not profit from being offered freedom of choice in the questions which they would answer. Conversely, the conclusion was that it would be worth while to experiment with situations in which students had no freedom of choice in examinations. A tentative investigation on these lines[12] confirmed that offering freedom of choice to these students, in these examinations, was not to their advantage.

This formative evaluation provided confirmation of a suspicion, and led to action. It was undertaken in a situation which called for more strength and authority than would have been the case in response to a mere suspicion in which there was little initial confidence – even on the part of the investigator.

- *Inform review and debate*: a formative evaluation of the interactions and the reactions of students during audio-conference calls opened up the whole possibility that affective, rather than cognitive, outcomes might be the most important for distant student learners in such situations.[13] That, in turn, led to consideration of the implications for telephone-conference tutorial design in terms of changed objectives and methods for the sessions.

Here there was no question of confirming a suspicion, nor was there a conclusion as such; there was merely the production of objective, and relevant, data for consideration, and subsequent action.

- *Discover unperceived needs*: we have already mentioned that the findings from interpersonal process recall generally lead to some shocked surprise on the part of tutors, and even students. This occurs when it emerges that there is a stark mismatch between the students' and tutor's perceptions of their interactions. But, as we hope we have already exemplified, it is usually a shock or surprise received by someone who is open to receive and to consider this type of feedback. In such circumstances, it is important that the reactions drawn from student subjects are honest, factually reported, and above all presented and considered in circumstances which are not threatening or embarrassing for the tutor. For in such cases the issue of the acceptability of the findings is not a real problem, in our experience.

- *Establish an unperceived need*: in this category, we consider problems in formative evaluation involving the work of those teachers who are *not* open to entertain doubts or reservations about their teaching. An evaluation must present such people with incontrovertible findings whose accuracy and relevance are without question. Here the evaluator should be in no doubt about the critical point to be made, while the confident teacher is equally in no doubt that all is well. The difficulty is to find a way of presenting data in order to make the point. For example, we recall the formative evaluation which revealed that, although the terminal examinations contained demanding questions and demanding part-questions, few marks were scored in the face of higher-level cognitive demands – even by the more able students. Marks were accrued by responding to questions and part-questions in which the demand was mundane, and often called for no more than regurgitation. When this was displayed in a form which made the point clearly, the unavoidable conclusion – for all, including the person concerned – was that no students displayed much competence in the objectives to which that teacher had previously claimed high commitment, and – by inference – teaching success.

What was urgently required here was to establish a hitherto unperceived need for improvement.

- *Change attitudes*: in another example of unperceived need, a teacher whose examinations consistently led to the failing of the majority of the students, maintained firmly at exam board meetings that his students were stupid, and that the marks in the other subjects must have been the result of soft marking or simple questions. A careful analysis was made of the performances of students in the examination in question. This showed that the questions appeared, from the student performance in answering them, to be of comparable difficulty, and that, while few students completed all of the stipulated questions, most students scored about 75 per cent of the available marks in what they had managed to attempt. The clear inference was that it was shortage of time, and not of ability, which was the root cause of low marks. The assertion of stupidity fell, although it was then open to the teacher to adopt a new hypothesis, of a slow rate of working! And the redesign of the examinations was established as an urgent need.

The role of this formative evaluation was not only to establish a need that had not been recognized as such, but to do so in a sufficiently powerful way so as to change the attitudes and assumptions underlying previous conclusions.

OUR GROUPING OF METHODS

In the following five chapters, we have collected together methods that have been of use to us and may be of use to you. Our grouping is to some extent arbitrary and personal. We have assembled ideas according to the purpose for which the method is, in our own experience, most useful; and since we recognize that some methods are useful for more than one purpose, we know that this subdivision may create difficulties for some readers, especially those with experience in this field.

Nonetheless, we group together methods that *primarily* obtain information about:

1. the immediate learning experience;
2. students' reactions that occurred during the learning experience;
3. the success of learners in achieving the intended learning outcomes;
4. student reactions *after* the experience.

We have deliberately left until third in our sequence those methods that inform teachers about the success of learners in achieving the intended learning outcomes. Our placing of the immediate learning experience as our first concern itself testifies to the importance that we place, as teachers, on the learning experiences that we create for our students. The next chapter, then, is followed by a chapter describing a linked group of methods, which enable us to obtain information about students' reactions during the learning experience. Only then do we move on to achievement of the learning outcomes, after which we include a section on a somewhat neglected type of data for formative evaluation, which is concerned with the student reactions *after* the experience – and perhaps long after it.

Conclusion

We hope that we have shown that:

- it will usually be best to use several methods of formative evaluation to provide a composite impression of the learning, teaching and assessment;
- methods should be chosen to provide the type of information that the evaluation requires;
- other factors, such as the way the information will be used, and by whom, are also of importance in the choice of method(s);
- it is desirable to give some thought to the values against which judgements will be made from evaluations;
- not all evaluations call for separate activity to generate data; some may use data that are already available, such as portfolios, learning journals and examination scripts.

Notes

1. See Method 3.5, pages 44 and 119.
2. See Method 4.2, pages 60 and 123.
3. See Method 6.4, page 84.
4. See Method 3.2, pages 39 and 115.
5. As discussed in Chapter 8, Question 10.
6. See Method 6.9, page 90.
7. See Perry, W (1970) *Forms of Intellectual and Ethical Development during the College Years: A scheme*, Holt, Rinehart and Winston, New York, who identified nine stages of development; see also Belenky, M F *et al* (1986) *Women's Ways of Knowing: The development of self, voice and mind*, Basic Books, New York.
8. See Method 6.4, page 84.

9. See Method 3.4, page 43.
10. See Method 4.2, pages 60 and 123.
11. For advice on analysis of data in general, see Robson, C (1993) *Real World Research: A resource for social scientists and practitioner-researchers*, pp 303–408, Blackwell, Oxford.
12. Cowan, J (1972) Is freedom of choice in examinations such an advantage?, *Technical Journal*, **10** (1), pp 31–32.
13. See Lee, M (1997) *Telephone tuition project report*, Open University in Scotland, Edinburgh.

CHAPTER 3

OBTAINING INFORMATION ABOUT THE IMMEDIATE LEARNING EXPERIENCE

In this chapter we are interested in methods of formative education which unearth information about the needs which students brought to the activity, or which emerged from the activity, or which were outstanding after the activity; the students' reactions to the structure of the teaching and learning; and their feelings about the process in general.

OUR DESCRIPTIONS

We concentrate on providing fairly full descriptions of methods, which you may wish to use yourself. We do that sometimes through examples where we can speak at first hand or as an observer of a method in use, and otherwise by descriptions in which we spell out what has to be done, so that you should not be left to improvise or fill in any blanks in the descriptions.

POSSIBLE GENDER DIFFERENCES

It is worth noting also that there is a strongly held view that objectivist, positivist and natural science modes of research tend to sit more naturally with men, and to occlude the women's perspective.[1] It has been argued persuasively that qualitative and reflexive methodologies might be more appropriate to feminist enquiry.[2] You may wish to have that thought firmly in mind, as you move on.

METHOD 3.1   SELF-CONFIDENCE SURVEYS

This comes chronologically at the beginning of our list, since it relates entirely to apprehensions which students can bring with them into their time of studying with you. Self-confidence surveys entail little more than a few direct questions to provide a rough indication of the confidence which students have in relation to this particular study, or to a skill or capability demanded within it.

Probably you will find the method most useful if you use it to focus on skills or abilities that you consider critical for success in the course or module. Having identified these, you compile simple questions asking for a rating of confidence under each heading – perhaps between 'very confident' and 'not at all confident', with a couple of intermediate stages. (You might alternatively give visual indicators of the range by drawing very smiling and very gloomy faces at each end.) You lay these out on a simple survey form, and ask the students to take a few minutes to consider their responses, and fill in the forms, which you then ingather as anonymous returns.

It will be of assistance to students who have low levels of self-confidence to learn the results of the enquiry, which will probably reveal to them that they are far from unusual. For the teacher, the information indicates aspects of the delivery that can profitably be tuned according to prevalent patterns of concern.

You might even wish to take this one stage further with a questionnaire which elicits interest in the various topics of the course – again informing the tutor who can then decide how to respond. However, this is hardly 'formative evaluation' as we have been using that concept!

Summary

We reiterate here a message in the model, for curriculum development to which we subscribe – namely that teaching should be a response to, and a support in respect of learning needs, either anticipated or declared. For that reason, our first priority here in formative evaluation is to determine, from the learning experience as it actually *is*, what needs are paramount for learners, and how they respond to the ways in which we have tried to support their learning.

METHOD 3.2   DYNAMIC LISTS OF QUESTIONS[3] – STUDYING LEARNING DURING AN EVENT

Example

I originally devised and used this exercise as one in which the students would draw up, before a learning activity, a list of the questions for which they hoped they would obtain answers by the end of the lesson or activity. Then, as the activity proceeded, they would gradually delete questions from it and keep a record of when the question no longer troubled them. For that reason my original title for the method was 'Diminishing lists of questions'.

In my searching for an understanding of the nature of learning and the learning experience, I soon discovered that the emergence of new questions and needs during the overall pattern of activity was as significant for the students as the elimination of declared needs. So I got them to *add* as well as to *delete* questions – since the emergence of new questions often testified to increased awareness and understanding.

For example, in one of the early runs, a maths student had begun by listing, *inter alia*, the question: 'How do you integrate by parts?'. Later, though, he had chosen to write: 'Now I know *how* to integrate by parts, but I don't know *when* to' – a need which, fortunately, the final part of the activity addressed for him. As a result of this type of volunteered information, I quickly encouraged students to declare their new questions and record progress with them. So I renamed the method 'Dynamic lists of questions', which seemed to be nearer to the optimum format for full feedback.

At the end of the activity, they would hand me their lists on which I could see the original questions (some of which had now been deleted), new questions which had been added, and questions outstanding when the activity concluded. Thus I had information about needs, and learning which had and had not met these needs.

As my familiarity with the method has increased, I find myself more often using it as an integral part of the structure for my activities. I identify perceived needs from lists of questions submitted beforehand, or contributed at the beginning. I design the programme so that these will receive attention. Then I 'mop up' at the end, hoping that there will be few outstanding or new questions in the outstanding agenda items which are declared, but nevertheless desiring to ensure that they all receive as much attention as possible.

The method, therefore, provides me with three different types of information:

1. I am informed, preferably with time to respond, about the priorities which students or participants have for an activity.

2. I find out (with time to respond, in at least some cases) what needs are still unfulfilled by the end of the activity.

3. I learn of questions that emerge for learners during the event, which is sometimes gratifying, and sometimes humbling (depending on the nature of the questions).

METHOD 3.3   OBSERVATIONS[4] – A METHOD WHICH DEPENDS ON THE ASSISTANCE OF A COLLEAGUE

It is as useful to observe others as to be observed – provided the purpose is for-mative, and not summative, and is to help in bringing about development in learning and teaching, and not to make a judgement on the quality of the teach-ing.[5]

We suggest that observers, at their most effective, should set out to obtain objective and accurate information about what is actually happening in a class, which can then be analysed and discussed. Observing colleagues may feel that they can usefully offer us advice on the quality of our course and teaching, or if we are up to date, relevant and teaching at the right level – in *their* opinion. We need to steer them clear of that summative and unhelpful temptation. It is probably best to plan our remit for their observations so that they objectively collect information that describes what *happens*. We can ask them to note any evidence, for example on whether:

- the students find that we have set out our aims and objectives in a clear and sound form;
- our choice of teaching methods is appropriate in that the learning outcomes are achieved;
- our choice of assessment methods is appropriate in that they demand the learning described in the learning outcomes;
- the quality of our materials is adequate in that students find them ef-fective and motivating in supporting their learning and develop-ment;
- the student workload is too heavy, too light or just right in relation to the course or module weighting;

Example

She (the tutor) had told me that she would set out to clear up difficulties relating to the next assignment, and would do so by working though something similar in small group activities in class. I, therefore, determined that it should be my primary concern to note the occurrence and content of every question or request for assistance relating to the assignment, or the class activity, when a student appeared to be having difficulty – or to need help, advice or reassurance. During the two-and-a-half-hour activity, there were three such requests – one for clarification, one seeking confirmation of an interpretation, and one asking for an explanation. At some time or another during the morning 9 of the 16 students indicated that they had already completed the assignment for which the activity had been designed to provide assistance. This was all the (sparse) evidence I could observe in the plenary work that related to the need that the session had apparently been designed to meet.

In the first half-hour I noted an apparent discrepancy in the participation of women and men, there being equal numbers in the individual groups. Thereafter I counted the numbers of male and female speakers making contributions in plenary. When selected by the (female) tutor to report back, approximately 75 per cent of the contributions were sought from men. When the groups chose their own speaker, 75 per cent of the contributions came from men. About 66 per cent of the contributions thereafter were by men. I, therefore, began to study the transactions within the small groups of four. In three of the four groups communication during group discussion was centred on, and usually led by, one of the women.

During the second plenary, I noted body movement in two of the four groups as the tutor spoke to the image on the overhead projector. I moved unobtrusively (I hoped) behind each of these two groups at the next two plenaries, and noted in each case that the tutor's position was such that much of the screen was obscured for those in groups on her right.

- the support available for students is appropriate, accessible and effective and the overall balance of the curriculum is apparent to the students.

Notice that these observations contain no explicit judgements, other than the decision about what to observe and report. They nevertheless contain considerable food for thought in respect of the appropriateness of the aims of the session, the experience for the women in the tutorial, and the use of the overhead projector.

Notice too that each item in the remit describes a request to the observer to search for evidence – or observations; but *not* to form and volunteer an opinion at that point. Subsequently, once you have assimilated this data you may, of course, and if you wish, discuss your interpretation of it, and your future intentions, with your colleague who carried out the observations for you.

Observers need to think carefully about how they will record observations. Making notes is an immediate action, and does not depend on memory. It calls for little or no preparation, and it allows a wide range of events and possibilities to be noted. However, it takes up time, during which other happenings are unlikely to be seen, or even heard properly, by the observer. It can generate notes that are difficult to decipher and expand; and it does not record the events themselves.

The use of a checklist or schedule to aid observation focuses attention, and leads to quickly made records in an appropriate form, which can be readily and comparably summarized and analysed; it also lessens the burden of recording while events occur. But it rigidly predetermines the focus of the observation, and depends on an observer who is familiar with the checklist, and who will be in difficulties when encountering events which it is difficult to accommodate in the checklist.

In contrast, making notes soon after the event is a good way to record overall impressions; for the observer is not distracted during the event and is thus less likely to miss significant items. But the events which have been observed are easily distorted in the memory and mental response; or they may even be forgotten. Considerable time must be devoted to this work *immediately* after the event. And, again, there is no record of events themselves.

Electronic recording provides a complete record, which can be replayed many times, and allows teachers to observe themselves and dispense with the involvement of a colleague. But in these circumstances most of us still find it difficult to be objective about the selection of features to observe, and our bias in the selection of the comprehensive recording of data is one in which our own behaviour figures prominently. Multiple replay of particular events can allow selection and subsequent study of a range of factors, such as a teacher's use of open-ended questions, eye contacts, hand gestures, and so on. But the process can be obtrusive, the quality of recording can be poor, and analysis is lengthy and time-consuming – and not always profitable. [6]

We tend to favour observations which concentrate on one aspect of the activity at a time, and then move to another feature – probably within one observation period though; this approach leads to quickly made and accurate notes; the observations originate partly from the brief given to us by the teacher, and partly from features which we notice during the observation, and on which we then concentrate for some time.

METHOD 3.4   CRITICAL INCIDENT TECHNIQUE

French[7] gives two neat examples in a paper in which he discusses the method and quotes a number of useful sources describing its origins.

Example 1

Within the constraints of normal course activity, four PGCE students from each of two small cohorts were interviewed and asked to recall times during the course when they had felt pleased, times when they had felt the reverse, activities in the programme which had been a good experience, activities which had seemed pointless, times when they had felt ineffective, and times when they were pleased with their performance. The audio tapes of the two-hour interviews were analysed for common themes. French reports that 'It was possible not only to gain a richer insight into the students' concerns, but also to suggest specific changes to course arrangements'.

Example 2

French then describes a similar formative evaluation of a four-year BEd course, where the size of the sample he required necessitated a more cost-effective way of ingathering the data. He used the same questions as before, but asked the students to write responses – anonymously – in group sessions. He states that 'The liveliness of what they wrote still gave more depth and feel of authenticity than is possible with traditional methods. The mismatch between some course intentions and the ways of working of some tutors could be reported in a dispassionate way, using clear examples'.

An observer, using this approach, may be briefed or unbriefed. If briefed, she is asked to look for and record specific categories of incident within a class session – perhaps the tutor's use of open-ended questions, or the peer interaction among students – to record in detail what actually happened, and to report this data to the tutor. If unbriefed, her colleague may simply have asked her to look for anything of interest or significance; and her observation may have led her to note, for example, the number of times the female students exchanged relevant comment among themselves as opposed to the number of times the male students did.

French gives further useful examples and detail of his questioning in the paper quoted above, which we recommend to you if you are inclined to use this approach.

METHOD 3.5 TALK-ALOUD PROTOCOLS[8]

Example – and the experience leading into it

Some years ago, I had my first serious encounter with the development and use by students of computer-assisted learning (CAL) software. My colleagues in the development team (in a department other than my own) showed me some of the materials which they had already produced, and asked me to assist with their formative evaluation. I played around with the software on my own, and formed a positive impression of it. I was interested to find out for the team the nature of the student learning experience.

However, I was influenced to some extent by my recent involvement as an external examiner for an educational PhD. This had presented me with the puzzling situation of two matched groups of students, both apparently using similar CAL programmes, but with the outcome that one group had acquired a deep and meaningful understanding of the concepts involved, while the other had operated at the level of playing a computer game – albeit successfully – and formed no understanding of the fundamental concepts whatsoever. There was no plausible explanation for that difference between the use of two apparently similar programs, nor – to my knowledge – was one ever found.

That experience had left me with a healthy curiosity about CAL, which impelled me to discover how students think and decide while carrying out learning tasks, and particularly so when this happens in novel situations. In my own research of conventional worked-example classwork[9] I had asked students to talk out their thoughts aloud into a tape-recorder as they solved problems which were a part of their study programme. And the findings which had emerged from the transcribed tapes had been a revelation to me.

So my inclination when I was asked to formatively evaluate the use of the CAL materials in maths was to recall the puzzle of the unexpected outcomes in the PhD project, and the wealth of information which protocols had provided for me, in my own teaching. Hence I decided to build upon my prior experience of protocol work. But since I then had no resource to undertake the laborious task of transcribing lengthy recordings, I went simply for 'talk-aloud' protocols.

I asked my colleagues to recruit trios of students who would be willing to assist in a modest enquiry where the findings would be anonymous. The students came from a class using the first CAL materials to have been produced and put into service. We met in a lecturer's staff room where a rather attractive buffet lunch awaited us. I explained how I wanted to work, and asked for questions – of which there were only a few minor ones – which I answered frankly. I gave the students a genuine opportunity to opt out at this point, if they so wished. None did.

We began. I sat one student at the terminal, with the other two at her shoulders. I told her to go into the package after the last that she had used in the CAL lab. She should then work on just as she would usually do but talking out her thoughts and feelings aloud as she did so, rather as a police driver in training talks out observations and thoughts and actions to describe the task while driving through traffic. As an explanation, I quickly took the machine into the program that I began to follow, illustrating what I was seeking as a style of commentary. I told her that she would work more slowly than usual, with this additional burden of providing a running commentary, but that this was not to worry her.

I asked the two other students to listen carefully, and try to understand what she was doing, and why. I asked them *not* to think about what they themselves would do, at any point in her progress; but to try to understand *her* reasoning and priorities. In particular, I charged the two observers to ask questions of the active student so that if she were to be called away to the telephone, one of the observers could sit down and carry on working with the materials *just as she would have done*. I have found this type of description of the task a helpful way of getting the listening students to try to empathize with the active one. I sat quietly in the background, and made notes of anything that seemed significant.

After 15–20 minutes, I got them to change places. Otherwise we followed the same procedure. I encouraged the second student to begin at the beginning, and not to pick up where the first had left off. Then we changed for a third and last time, and did the same again.

I now came out of the background and summarized what I had heard and noted. I reported that it had seemed to me that:

- certain points mattered quite strongly to at least one of you (and I listed examples, such as a tediously repeated explanation, and a welcome feedback on inaccurate responses);
- there were points on which you disagreed, or worked or reacted in different ways (and again I listed them);
- there were certain points or tasks or instructions that created problems for you, other than the difficulty of the material (another list);
- these features of the program were the ones that you praised or enthused about (a final list).

We discussed my lists, amended them perhaps a little, but it should only have been a little – if I had been doing my job effectively. I then asked if I might pass on this information to the team without mentioning names. The students were always happy for me to do so.

Let me quote one example from each of my early lists, to illustrate the type of information I was passing to the course team:

1. One particular jump from using the keyboard (in use for a while) to using the mouse (once) and then straight back to the keyboard was universally and intensely loathed, and – as the team later told me – readily avoidable.

2. The woman student 'cheated' her way quickly to answers or correction on a first pass through the material, and then worked backwards or on a second pass. And she learnt better and quicker that way than the others, or than when she behaved as the team had intended.

3. One set of options created problems of interpretation, through ambiguities.

4. The use of moving diagrams to present some of the problems and certain explanations of answers was universally praised, with encouraging examples of the ways in which the diagrams had assisted assimilation.

I passed all of this on to the course team, who assembled an amalgam of responses from several trios and formulated questions which they then wished to ask of the entire class group and discuss with them. All of this led to appreciable and beneficial changes in the style of the next CAL materials to be produced – and to a greater amount of gratuitous and volunteered suggestions on future programs.

In the form which we have described, each student should be able to remain anonymous. That is not the case when individuals talk through a procedure on tape, which is then to be analysed. The variant we have described, therefore, has the advantage of avoiding, or at least reducing, the effect of inhibition.

Note, incidentally, that students' protocols are likely to be markedly individual, and hence difficult to summarize and compare in the usual ways. For that reason, however, they provide thought-provoking insights into the extent and nature of individuality in learning, and are a splendid source of data about how that individuality leads different students to tackle problem-solving situations, and to encounter their own particular difficulties.

METHOD 3.6   JOURNALS, DIARIES AND LOGS – WHICH WE REGARD AS DIFFERENT

We would defend to the death your right to use any of these everyday words in our heading here with your own specialized meaning. For our own part, in this present educational context, our use will be as follows.

If students, or teachers, keep a factual and precisely detailed record of what they are doing each day and evening, as far as teaching, learning and assessment are concerned, we call that a *log*. If they keep a less comprehensive factual account of what they see as the important events of each day, without necessarily recording timings but probably with some comment and even reflection, we call that a *diary*. If they engage in their writing up what is mainly analytical and evaluative thinking, mulling over events and their implications, with the emphasis on the reflection and not on the description of the events upon which they are reflecting, then we refer to that as a *journal*. We hope you will be able to adopt that usage within the covers of this book.

Journals: a different origin of a method for formative evaluation

Elsewhere in this text we have described many methods of formative evaluation which commence with the intention of obtaining helpful information about teaching, learning and assessment. These approaches, like the dynamic list of questions,[10] often progress to becoming an integral part of the teaching and learning activities, where almost instantaneous feedback becomes more and more an embedded feature within the activities. The progression in these cases is from evaluation as a separate effort, to evaluation as an integrated part of the teaching and learning activity.

Journals are, in our experience, an example of the reverse process, for they originate as a vital form of teaching and learning activity which naturally generates learning and unearths information. Some of this information can then be used readily within formative evaluation, merely by separating it out, collecting it and then responding to it. The progression in this case is from a learning and developmental activity *into* formative evaluation, almost as a by-product.

A specific remit to journal writers

Example

I find it useful to explain the journalling task to students – and teachers – who have never kept a reflective journal before, by advising that they follow a three-stage process. First, I suggest that they describe, briefly and certainly in no more than a paragraph of normal length, the most significant event of that part of their recent or current learning experience to which the journal entry will relate. Next, I suggest that, after careful thought, they identify a question – just one, and one which can be expressed adequately in a sentence – for which they don't yet have an answer, and whose answer would be of use to them, in advancing their learning or development. Then, last of all, I ask them to think and write either about how to obtain an answer to that question, or about what the various possible answers might be.

This type of journal entry directly generates valuable and current data about the learning needs with which learners are engaged; or, in the case of journals kept by teachers, of the current challenges in curriculum presentation and development with which the teachers are grappling. In a second-level module on personal development planning, several students, for example, wrestled in their journal entries with issues of time-management and prioritizing; that need being known, tutorial action could readily be provided. In a learning journal kept by a student on a Level 3 course in engineering design, the writer identified difficulty with the selection of effective ways to develop certain conceptual understanding and used the journal exercise as the first step towards finding a promising solution. Having identified needs which had not been dealt with in the course, she then took steps to bring this to the attention of her tutor.

Such journal entries directly identify individual needs that have not as yet been satisfactorily resolved by the programme – though they do not do so according to a representative or statistically defensible pattern. This, however, then makes it possible for these needs to be investigated and checked for frequency of occurrence, and so to receive attention either within the class programme or individually – as appropriate.

Another form of remit for journalling

Reflective learning journals are presently also used as a component of that form of facilitated learning which follows the Kolb Cycle (see Figure 3.1) in pursuit of the development of abilities,[11] and especially of the higher-level cognitive and interpersonal abilities which are of growing importance in higher education.

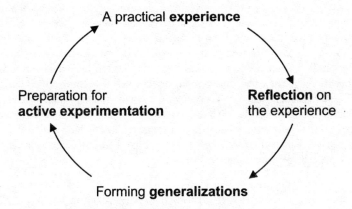

Figure 3.1   *A freely adapted version of the Kolb Cycle*

Students seek valid generalizations from particular experiences, and they actively experiment with these generalizations in facing new challenges. They are asked, and usually required, to engage in the far from simple task of committing their reflections to paper, or to an electronic file. These reflective journals often come at this point to tutors for facilitative comment, so the opportunity to profit from them, with input to formative evaluation of the provision, occurs almost naturally.[12]

Such journals should contain first-hand personal accounts of what has been learnt, or not learnt, from the teaching and learning activities within the programme; and they should contain constructive reflections on the difficulties which students confront, and cannot overcome, as they seek to put their learning to good use. A typical journal, in our experience, will contain a helpful – and balanced – mix of learning and needs, a review of what has just been done, and anticipation of what lies immediately ahead.

As in the previous example, the next journal example directly identified individual needs[13] that had not as yet been satisfactorily resolved by the programme – though it did not identify them according to a representative or statistically defensible pattern. However, it made it possible for these needs to be considered and to receive attention when discovered to be widespread. It also, unlike the first example, provided useful information about learning progress and teaching success, which was at variance with the teachers' intuitive judgement, and was something on which they could build with confidence.

Example

In my Level 1 course on problem-solving, many students reported the 'blue flash' experiences which they had had, in seeing a more purposeful way to tackle problems, all occasioned by one particular workshop activity. Until we received that feedback (which came within 48 hours of the event) we teachers had noted with concern what we had taken to be total bewilderment on the part of students. But we now realized that our class had left the event quietly and pensively because they had encountered much that they judged was useful. There had been little or no confusion in their minds. When we read the journals, as commentators, we learnt something which surprised us about the effectiveness of our workshop; and our tentative intention to 'try again' in a different way was, therefore, replaced by a firm – and informed – resolve to build upon the reported assimilation.

In the same course, but one week later, one journal – and only one in a class of over 50 students – reported that problem-solving had gone well in the days following the workshop. However the journal writer was still sometimes at a loss for a strategy when he had tried everything he could think of, had made no progress and didn't know what to do next. His journal clearly identified his need to develop the ability to resolve the type of impasse that sometimes occurred in his problem-solving. Thus a declared, but perhaps unrepresentative, need emerged from this journal. I went to the class, described the situation as I have described it here, and asked how many others had had the same difficulty on occasions. A quick show of hands confirmed that more than half the class had the same need, although they had not identified it in their journalling. The declared and confirmed need became an objective for the next activity which we arranged for this class in interdisciplinary studies – as a result of the formative feedback we gleaned from this one journal entry and our subsequent enquiry.

Logs

Logs are a good example of a helpful component of formative evaluation, which is nevertheless usually only the first step in a two-stage process. A log should record what has happened, and so it is a way of linking information and action. Mainly the entries in a log describe what students and teachers have been doing, and how long they have spent on different aspects of that activity. So logs, in our experience, can prompt you to enquire systematically and objectively about certain aspects of your teaching and the learning it supported in an attempt to capitalize on effectiveness, while responding to signals that some activity may have been ineffective.

In a log, you (the teacher) might record on a weekly basis or less:

- the programme;
- attendance;
- curious or unexpected behaviour or responses;
- apparent successes;
- feedback;
- actions planned.

In associated logs, your students can record on a weekly basis or less:

- their activities within the programme or related to it;
- time spent under various headings;
- learning progress or successes;
- difficulties.

This information, provided it is comprehensive and reliable and is objectively analysed, can be a thought-provoking source of often surprising information about:

- how much, and how little, time students and teachers spend on certain components of the programme;
- the order in which students and teachers tackle tasks in the programme;
- how soon (or late) students respond to assignment tasks; and how late (or early) they begin to prepare submissions;
- the time taken in accessing resources, and in resolving problems with the aid of support services.

Keeping logs is a difficult discipline, so a request to students that they maintain a log for a short period (even 2–3 days) is more likely to lead to accuracy than would a demand for prolonged log-keeping over several weeks. The latter can readily lead to retrospective record-keeping, which owes more than is desirable to wishful thinking and creative writing. The simpler you can make the log-sheet, the more likely the students are to keep records and to keep them accurately. Additionally, if you can show an example, even a manufactured one, it will help them to know what is expected of them.

Anonymity can be retained, and your own time saved, if the analyses can be undertaken within small student groups and reported back via a snowball or pyramid approach.[14] However, the facts which logs *should* record can concern more than the log-keeper may be willing to reveal of omissions, procrastination and even inadequacy. Anonymity, even to other students, is, therefore, desirable if a log is likely to be seen by more than the writer – and it should be known from the outset that individuals will be so protected. Perhaps the most powerful use of the log is when the log-writer is prompted in some way to reflect and conclude directly on what the log itself tells her or him.

There are two further points we would emphasize in the use of data from logs. They should be triangulated or cross-checked for accuracy; and above all they should be sought in a way which only asks for data which will be of use. Too many logs record too much.

Angelo and Cross have a further example,[15] which they call Diagnostic Learning Logs. In these, they ask learners to record what they learnt, and how effective that learning was, according to a simple proforma which is explained by means of a sample compilation. The students are then assisted to identify strengths and weaknesses in their learning, and to report them. This encourages students to self-assess their progress, and to become more proactive learners. It also alerts the teacher to the students' progress in attaining metacognitive skills. However, there is a danger that this style can demoralize students due to its concentration on weaknesses.

Diaries

A diary is usually an intensely personal record. Most diaries, which are more than logs, abound in subjective comments of importance to the writers, and reveal much about them. For that reason most diary writers would be loathe to allow access to the diary by another reader.

Example

I was required, as a schoolchild, to keep a diary for each day of the year. At the year's end, I had to look back over the year, with the assistance of my diary entries, and record what significant experiences it contained, and what progress I had made. What surprises there were in some of these entries of less than a year's standing; and what noteworthy incidents I discovered to have faded from my memory in the short space of a year! How glad I was that this system, which I did not understand, did not ask me to allow anyone else to read my diary.

I still keep a diary, on occasions – and especially when I take on a new teaching task. I record my impressions – and feelings – at the time, especially in the early stages. And I find it useful to go back, at the end of the term or the academic year, to be reminded of these early impressions and reactions which may well have faded from my mind or, more often, have become distorted in my memory.

The usefulness of the diary, then, in higher education practice and in particular in relation to formative evaluation, is that it can be a source document to which a student or teacher returns for prompts about matters which might otherwise not be recalled. We could not ourselves envisage the use of a personal diary, as we have used that description, for other than personal and private use.

METHOD 3.7 SELF-REVIEW

Example

For many years I operated a learning unit in which students learnt, mainly individually, with the assistance of pre-recorded resource materials.[16] It was my aim to provide an environment and support materials that would leave tutors free to attend to individual difficulties, and needs which were somewhat special. It, therefore, perturbed me if we spent time attending to the same enquiry or request from more than, say, six students in a class of 50–90 students. And so we kept a record of frequent enquiries, demands and requests, in what we called a 'post-mortem file' whose primary concern was with needs with which the resource-based learning might not be coping adequately.

As we taught, managed and marked coursework, we had other occasions to think that perhaps the materials or the approach should be changed in the following year. We worked with students, we listened, we watched them and we deduced accordingly – perhaps not always correctly. A short note along the lines of our thoughts for change could also be jotted down, and popped into the burgeoning post-mortem file. We told students of the file, and asked them to contribute to it if they felt that they could identify any possibility for improvement, or any weakness in the provision which merited our attention.

Each August, in the interim period between academic years when there was an opportunity to make considered revisions to materials, or to the range of materials on offer, one of us would empty out the bundle of notes on their assorted pieces of paper, and conduct a preliminary analysis, to see if any endorsed messages emerged, or if there were discrepancies which merited attention in our review. Aided by this, we were able to consider the contents of the post-mortem file and the implications of what it contained. Usually this led to such revisions as improvements in the detail of some of the resource materials – a better slide, a clearer diagram, and an extra diagram or a change in wording; or to additional materials – where remedial explanations had been needed by a significant minority; and to the omission or radical curtailing of some explanatory sequences which most students had found unnecessary and tedious.

Notice that the features which made this self-review worthy of being described as formative were the systematic collection of data, in the form of comments, observations and suggestions *at the time*, the objective analysis of that data, which led to some being set on one side, and the purposeful reaction to the messages which the team then took from the data.

METHOD 3.8   COLLECTING COMMENTS FROM GROUPS

It is common to obtain information about the nature of the immediate learning experience by asking questions of groups of students in the midst of their (teaching and) learning activity. There are five widely used ways of collecting comments from this source:

1. *Buzz groups*: here students are divided into small groups to address a task or question, the title coming from the ensuing 'buzz' of conversation. The interaction during the buzzing tends to provoke contributions that are reactions to what has just been said by someone else. The tutor then takes comment evenly from each of the groups in turn, circling again to take one further comment from any group which has one, until there is nothing fresh to add.

2. *Snowball technique*: for group accumulation of comment. Here students usually start off by addressing a question individually, then working in pairs, and finally in quartets. The starting point of individual work gives an opportunity for everyone to gather their thoughts, thus not allowing vociferous people to swamp the contributions – and the coverage is better.

3. *Pyramid technique*: this is a variant of the snowball, which goes in one step from individuals to small groups of four or six.

4. *Interrupted lectures*: without warning, the lecturer interrupts a lecture to ask the students questions about process, such as how much they were, or were not concentrating, what notes or records they were keeping at the time of this interruption, and if they were making any links between this new content and anything they had learnt previously. Allow a minute or two for them to write down their reflective responses; then proceed with the class, with probably only one more such interruption, with the same questions. As the students leave, they put the sheets with their comments into a basket or box. The information gained anonymously is of the way students process the information presented in class, and how they listen. Note, though, that it probably disturbs these behaviours by encouraging reflection and self-monitoring – though to good purpose.

5. *Chain notes*: the lecturer formulates a question – perhaps about what students are focusing their attention on. This question is written on the

outside of an envelope that is passed round the class, to be answered quickly by each student in turn, according to the circumstances when the envelope reaches them. Each student writes his or her response on a slip of paper, and posts it into the envelope. Provided the students are honest, which they should have been asked to be, the reactions can be pertinent and informative and may be an early-warning device!

Such structured discussion with a class of students avoids 'questionnaire fatigue', and allows the time for amplification and clarification. However, it takes time, it can be difficult to handle in large classes, and it needs sensitive and skilled chairing or facilitating. Most importantly, the quality and focus of the comment it elicits is heavily dependent on the nature of the task or question given to the groups, and the extent to which they then address it. We would commend the type of question used in the critical incident method[17] as a starting point when soliciting comments from groups; and we would advise that comment be formulated and passed on as soon as possible after the event(s) to which it refers.

Notes

1. See Oakley, A (1981) Interviewing women; a contradiction in terms, in *Doing Feminist Research*, ed H Roberts, Routledge and Kegan Paul, London.
2. Chodorov, N J (1996) Seventies questions for thirties women; Some nineties reflections, in *Feminist Social Psychologies*, ed S Williams, pp 21–50, Open University Press, Milton Keynes. Cf Shields, S A and Crowley, J J, Appropriating questionnaires and rating scales for a feminist psychology: a multi-method approach to gender and emotion, in the same volume, pp 218–32.
3. See Appendix (page 115), for a more complex variant of the method, applicable if you want to investigate the impact which teaching in individual sections has had on the overall pattern of learning.
4. For a useful overview, again see Robson, C (1993) *Real World Research: A resource for social scientists and practitioner-researchers*, pp 190–226, Blackwell, Oxford. For further details, see Appendix (page 117).
5. Graham Gibbs, in the draft materials for the Open University course H852, *Course Design in Higher Education* (forthcoming), goes so far as to suggest that our first source of data for formative evaluation, as for feedback, is the evidence of our own eyes and ears. We would happily go along with that – provided it is taken as the *first* source.
6. For suggestions about observing in various ways inside classrooms, see Angelo, T A and Cross, K P (1992) *Classroom Assessment Techniques*, 2nd edn, Jossey-Bass, San Francisco.
7. See French, T (1992) *Data for evaluation tapping significant experience – an approach to the critical incident technique*, Proceedings of the CNAA Conference on Evaluating the quality of the student experience, Council for National Academic Awards, London. Cf also Flanagan, J C (1954) The critical incident technique, *Psy-*

chological Bulletin, **15** (4), pp 327–58.

8. For further detail on this method, see Appendix (page 119).

9. See Cowan, J (1977) Individual approaches to problem solving, in *Aspects of Educational Technology*, vol X, Kogan Page, London; (1980) Improving the recorded protocol, *Programmed Learning and Educational Technology*, **17** (3), pp 160–63.

10. See Method 3.2, page 39.

11. See Kolb, D (1984) *Experiential Learning*, Prentice Hall, New York.

12. For a case study of use of journals, see Cowan, J, *Education for Capability in Engineering Education*, D.Eng thesis, Heriot-Watt University, Edinburgh.

13. In another form of journal, a more straightforward task may call for analytical reflection – answering the question: 'How do I do this?' when posed about a process which is a common demand in the area of study. It may then be possible to encourage students to build upon this reflection, by comparing notes, swapping ideas and reporting outstanding difficulties – which can then receive your attention.

14. See Method 3.8, page 54.

15. See Angelo, T A and Cross, K P (1993) *Classroom Assessment Techniques*, 2nd edn, pp 311–15, Jossey-Bass, San Francisco (note that the first edition of this work has the authors in reverse order – Cross and Angelo).

16. See Cowan, J, Morton, J and Bolton, A (1973) An experimental learning unit for structural engineering studies, *The Structural Engineer*, **51** (9), pp 337–40.

17. See Method 3.4, page 43, and the work by French referred to there.

CHAPTER 4

Obtaining Information About Immediate Reactions During the Learning Experience

In this chapter we focus – with a slight difference from the previous group of methods – on approaches which unearth, with hindsight, reactions which occurred during the event. Our first example, for instance, is about identifying student reactions to a tutor's comments on written assignments when that work is returned to them.

METHOD 4.1 IDENTIFYING STUDENTS' CONSTRUCTS IN RELATION TO THEIR LEARNING[1]

Example

The following passage gives the context in which we first came across the use of an adapted form of Kelly's Repertory Grid[2] for this purpose. We suggest that, as you read, you think about how to translate this approach into one which you could use in a large class, in a conventional setting, for determining a variety of student reactions.

I expressed to colleagues my interest in finding out about the effectiveness of my comments to my students, when I wrote in the margins of the assignments which they submitted to me. I was encouraged by John and Judith to experiment with an adapted version of Kelly's Repertory Grid technique, with which I was already familiar in its conventional form.

In this pilot study, I marked my students' work in the usual way, and added my usual type of comment. When I had completed this, I numbered the comments, in a way that I felt distinguished discrete comments. I then phoned John who had agreed to act as a 'messenger'. He picked up the assignments from me, for direct return to the students, instead of following the normal Open University practice which routes assignments via the main university offices at Milton Keynes.

I had previously explained to the students what I wanted to do, and why. And I had obtained their (ready) agreement to collaborate. The messenger was, therefore, able to telephone the students, arrange a time for delivery, and turn up on the doorstep – asking each student to deal with the package as if it had been returned, as usual, via the postal service.

After the student had assimilated the contents of the envelope, the messenger explained the detail of the method. He indicated that he would give the student the numbers of three comments and ask them to refer to these and to separate that trio into a pair and a singleton, according to a feature which mattered to the student, which was possessed either by the pair but not the singleton, or vice versa. For example, the student might differentiate between two comments that offered encouragement, and one that contained criticism.

Once the student had decided on the split, and told the messenger the factor on which division had been based, the messenger took the student down the remainder of the comments, asking which had, and had not, the feature which had just been identified. Which ones offered encouragement, in effect? A tick went against the comment(s) that had that factor; a cross if it was absent.

The messenger now chose a further trio, all of which either had, or had not, been ticked. He then asked the student to further differentiate between this group, as before. The student might note that one gave an explanation for praising or encouraging, while the other two merely said 'Good point' or 'Well explained'. Again the remaining comments were ticked or crossed, according to whether I had or had not given an explanation in my comment, whatever it was.

And so the process proceeded – until it proved difficult to find trios with the same pattern of crosses and ticks. The messenger than asked the student if there were any other features of comments which mattered to them. Often this question elicited another one or two, which could go in as headings in the table of results, and were then checked off against each comment.

Finally the messenger asked the student which type of comment was most helpful – and why. Interestingly rather more than half favoured the positive comment, provided it was accompanied by a reason: 'This was a good explanation, *because you* …'. One student even said firmly that he would rather have one such *explained* piece of praise than half a dozen unexplained positive comments. In the same class group, however, there were rather less than half (but still a significant number) who preferred instead to be told what they had done poorly, *together with* an explanation of what was wrong with that, or how it could be improved.

I was now in a position to comment to each student next time according to *their* reports of their preferred style. I had also learnt that some of my comments provoked an undesired, and unexpected, negative reaction, which gave me food for thought about revising my style. And I realized that yet other comments were not understood – which again was useful feedback.

In the following years, after this pilot, I was able to devise ways to get my students to use an adaptation of this method themselves, to tell me which kind of comments they found most useful, and how they were responding – without the costly assistance of a colleague to act as messenger.[3]

Uncovering what are called personal constructs was the initial purpose of the tutor's use of this method. The underlying principle here is that people view the world in different ways, and categorize it according to personal constructs which may be distinctly individual in character.

In another such enquiry, when asked to compare course modules (rather than comments) in the way described above, one student came up with headings for the columns in the grid which described cognitive content – numerate or not, creative or analytical, researched knowledge or postulated theory, and so on. Another described modules in terms of features of the teaching styles and learning demands. Yet another compared the modules in terms of what did and did not appear to matter in the learning – and how she rated these values. Such personal constructs reveal a great deal about individual responses to, and needs within, the learning experience. Hence the method can be used in more areas than assignment commenting to unearth students' world views – or rather their educational world views.

In every case, the method concentrates on individuals and individual perspectives, which matter for precisely that reason, Therefore, the findings should only be summarized with caution, since they may not justify generalizations. The method can be time-consuming, and it certainly has limited application to large groups, although anonymized findings can be used as a basis for discussion or for a questionnaire. Depending on the relationships which the student has with the teacher and enquirer, the method can even be perceived as threatening, and it is certainly easy for the enquirer, or teacher, to misinterpret the findings.

Despite that, we see considerable potential in the use of Kelly's Repertory Grid in situations where students carry out their own analyses, and report, from snowball or pyramid groups, the range of constructs which they have identified. We have used self-managed Kelly analysis to good effect, with Level 1 students who have never before encountered the method, in classes of 80–100, with pyramid group reporting. Our enquiry was to ascertain from these students the features which, in their judgement, characterized effective teaching.

METHOD 4.2   INTERPERSONAL PROCESS RECALL[4]

Example

The original technique, which we describe as IPR, was one that had been used widely, most notably in the training of counsellors.[5] We decided to try radically adapting it for use with a group of tutor counsellors who were working with first-year Open University students of very varied educational backgrounds and ability. We then extended its use to other teaching situations when we found how rich a source of valued data it could prove to be.

One evening, with the agreement of a group of social science students and their tutor, we brought a video-camera and a replay machine to their tutorial. One of us set up the camera as unobtrusively as possible in the corner of the room, started it as the tutorial began, and left the room. The camera was directed at the tutor, not at the students; and the students were assured of this.

At the end of the tutorial, we asked for two student volunteers to spend about 20 minutes each with us, 'unpacking' their learning experience of the evening. We reassured them (genuinely) that when we had ourselves had the experience of 'being unpacked', we had found it extremely interesting and in no way embarrassing. Taking each student in turn, one of us who was acting as enquirer sat with the student to watch the replay of a short part of the tape of the session. Explaining again that this was to get feedback about the effect of the teaching, not of the learning, the enquirer began replaying the tape, stopping every 20 seconds or so, or when the student's eyes or face indicated that there had been something of interest happening. At each pause, the enquirer asked what was happening for the student – what feelings or thoughts she was recalling – and attempted to take brief notes of the rich flow of data which was prompted by the visual trigger of this recent experience.

We managed to take recall from these two students before it was time for them to return home.[6] We then reported back the notes we had made to the tutor for his information, as a basis on which he could then make judgements about his effectiveness and any changes he wished to make.

One of the most vivid and useful bits of feedback from this session was from the first minutes of this tutorial. It was the tutor's habit to talk to the group as they arrived, mixing social pleasantries with enquiries about progress and dealing incidentally, and naturally in a somewhat erratic order, with any questions or problems which were raised by one arrival after another, as having come up during the week which had elapsed since the previous tutorial. Once the students had all arrived and were settled, the tutor checked that they were ready for him to move on to the agenda for the evening, and before so doing gave a brief and neatly organized extempore summary of the main points which had emerged in the 'warm-up' period. We focused on this summary, expecting the data to provide endorsement of effective practice.

To our surprise, the IPR data at this point revealed intense frustration on the part of the students. They told us that the summary had just served to prompt further ideas and questions, which the tutor then inadvertently stifled by moving on. Questioned as to why they had not raised the matters which then troubled them, the students explained that they would not, for the world, have ever have mentioned this directly to the tutor. They were *so* appreciative of the effort and enthusiasm he put into their tutorial, and his care to ask about outstanding problems and difficulties, that they felt they could never have said anything which could possibly be interpreted as a criticism. Once this had come to light through the IPR-stimulated recall, though, the tutor simply changed his routine to continue asking again, after his summarizing, if that had raised further questions, and only moved on to fresh topics after he had mopped up.

This was a typical example of the kind of insight that this method has provided throughout our relatively widespread use of it. The video prompt releases a rich flow of the kind of jumbled thoughts and feelings, relevant and irrelevant, which we all are aware of experiencing when we are in the midst of such situations, but which we find it difficult to recall later in any detail. The insights which the technique gives has alerted many tutors, as well as ourselves, to aspects of our style, to turns of phrase, and to habits of organization, which could be simply and easily changed to make us more responsive to students' needs.

The most interesting findings tend to be what we call 'mismatches', where the tutor's perception of what is happening turns out to be totally, or at least significantly, at variance with the student's. A typical example was when one of us was trying to help a student with a difficult mathematical procedure. The pair were getting along fine, but suddenly the student went very quiet. The tutor, not having the faintest idea why this had happened, and suspecting that something which had been said or done had upset the student, was just about to find a tactful way to close the session and allow the poor student to escape. What the video feedback unearthed in recall, however, was that the student was concentrating intensely at that moment, thinking how sympathetic and supportive the tutor was being by just leaving space and time for thinking, and feeling on the point of overcoming what had until then been an important learning difficulty. Feedback in this case gave a tutor who had tended to worry about, and even curtail, awkward silences the confidence to keep quiet on the next occasion, to trust that the reason for silence was not negative, and perhaps even to enquire of the student in due course about what had been in her thoughts – an important insight and development for this tutor.

We have found that IPR is a very rich source of a type of data which we have not been able to obtain in any other way – information about many of the thoughts and feelings during the event, which give real and deep insights into the whole range of the learning experience. Experienced enquirers can use it to focus precisely on particular strategies or passages of presentation, and arrive at a detailed formative description of experience. The method leads to an intriguing return visit by the subjects, students *and* tutors, to recent memories which are recalled (in most cases) with startling clarity and detail.

In recruiting and briefing students for this form of formative evaluation, it is worth ensuring that tutor and enquirer have each been subjects themselves in a genuine and recent recall experience, and can speak to that experience – probably and naturally with examples – when they are explaining the method and enquiry to the students. Make sure that you set aside enough time for the enquiry sessions – this can be quite time-consuming. For that reason, it is a method which you would only use occasionally, and you should not overestimate the length of the fragment of the session on which you can obtain recall. A five-minute fragment will take at least 25 minutes to 'unpack' with even a relatively reticent student.

We have found that it is adequate to use the method thoroughly just once in the life of a particular class group with a few students from that class group. Even that is sufficient to establish the interest of the teacher in a deeper and more detailed level of feedback about the nature of the learning experience, describing the effect the teacher is having on that. This exchange then establishes a climate in which such feedback is subsequently provided quite easily and informally, without the need for further IPR sessions.

You should be careful to distinguish this activity from micro-teaching, which is a situation where the performance of the teacher/tutor is recorded and then constructively analysed and discussed. However useful that approach may be, it calls for a different approach, and leads to different outcomes. People can easily confuse IPR with micro-teaching, and miss the strengths of both methods as a result.

METHOD 4.3   JOURNALS – AGAIN!

Example

In my use of journals, I have tended to favour the style in which the journals are completed and submitted weekly for comment by a tutor. I then comment in what I have described to myself and others as a Rogerian style, following the philosophy of Carl Rogers[7] in attempting to empathize, display congruence, and have unconditional positive regard for the writer. Where I think a *non sequitur* is evident, I will ask gently if the writer saw how to get from the first to the second part of the argument. Where a conclusion seems unjustified, I point out that no evidence had been quoted to support what the writer had concluded, and wonder if that could be produced. Where a strong expression of feelings is tabled, I attempt to empathize with source of feeling.

In this context, I carefully monitor my comments, and the reasons that I made them. I draw up a table in which I list down the left-hand side the types of cause which prompt me to comment – *non sequitur*, unjustified conclusion, and so on. Then across the top of the table I put the type of response – a question, pointing out what I see or read in the text, a reflective comment, and so on. My purpose in this self-monitoring is to be aware of my commenting approach and to monitor consistency and patterns within it. But it has a by-product for formative evaluation.

I can learn a lot from the occasions that prompted me to comment, if they occur frequently. Quite often the journals for a difficult week are rich in reports of feelings – of what has made the writers angry, worried or sad; or exultant, confident or grateful. Sources of strong negative and positive feelings are richly thought-provoking information for aspects of teaching and learning worthy of attention as a consequence of this formative evaluation.

Summary

Reactions during the learning experience are mainly affective – they are expressed as welcome or unwelcome feelings, provoked (often strongly) by what we have planned for the students. In most cases it will cause us to ponder if we find that we have caused students to be angry or worried; for if so, we will usually wish to reconsider the design of our programme or activity. In some cases, however, we may be pleased to learn that students with unperceived needs[8] are angry to discover that they are not as perfect as they had fondly imagined; for progress is more likely to occur from that starting point. In some cases we will be better able to plan the detail of our facilitation more helpfully if we know what worries students – about the challenge, for example, of moving up the Perry scale.[9]

Reactions to the learning experience are important data for formative evaluation. They *may*, however, be difficult to handle. Often they can confront us with the powerful consequences of our teaching activity, of which the teacher who merely instructs is usually blissfully unaware, but to which an immature or sensitive teacher may well overreact. Objectivity is something we must seek to ensure, perhaps by testing out the combination of the evidence and the appropriateness of our reaction to it on a detached and sensible peer.

Notes

1. Details of this method, in a face-to-face version for use with a large class, are given in the Appendix (page 121).
2. Kelly, G (1955) *The Psychology of Personal Constructs*, Norton, New York.
3. See Weedon, E M (1994) *An investigation into using self-administered Kelly analysis*, Project Report 94/5, Open University in Scotland, Edinburgh.
4. A detailed account of our particular version of this method can be found in the Appendix (page 123).
5. See Kagan, N (1975) Influencing human interaction: eleven years with IPR, *The Canadian Counsellor*, 9 (2), pp 74–97. Details of the attempts made by the Open University in Scotland to extend the numbers of students providing immediate recall are to be found in Cowan, J *et al* (1990) The formative evaluation of study skills workshops, *Report of the Annual Conference of Scottish Educational Research Association*.
6. For using this method with students in connection with telephone tuition, see Cowan, J (1994) *Telephone Interpersonal Process Recall*, Project Report 1994/1, Open University in Scotland, Edinburgh.
7. See Rogers, C R (1967) *On Becoming a Person*, Constable, London.
8. Garry, A M and Cowan, J (1987) To each according to his needs, *Aspects of Educational Technology*, Vol XX, pp 333–37, Kogan Page, London. In this paper, the writers point out that needs can be expressed, felt, unformulated or unperceived – and that the approaches to be used for identifying these, and for dealing with them, should vary markedly.
9. See Perry, W (1970) *Forms of Intellectual and Ethical Development during the College Years: A scheme*, Holt, Rinehart and Winston, New York.

CHAPTER 5

OBTAINING INFORMATION ABOUT LEARNING OUTCOMES

METHOD 5.1   CONCEPT MAPPING

Example

I am an Open University tutor teaching a 30-point course. This is equivalent to a quarter of the workload for a full-time student. On this essentially distance-learning course there is not much tutorial contact time available for my students and myself, so our time together is precious and must not be wasted.

The course, which is *Homer: Poetry and Society*, covers a wide discipline area – the Homeric texts themselves, together with study of oral poetry and development of the skills of literary analysis, the archaeological record of the period (with substantial video footage supplied on tape), and comparative texts of war poetry from the early 20th century. In the times we have available together, it is critically important for me to gain sound insight into what are the learning needs for my particular group of students – what they are finding as blocks and barriers, what is enthusing them but needs development, and how successful my design of tutorial sessions has been in progressing their understanding.

At the beginning of the first tutorial, I suggest that we set aside the last 15 minutes of each face-to-face tutorial for review. The students and I will each draw our own concept map of what they have learnt, or in my case what I believe I have covered, during the session. Students are often unfamiliar with this kind of activity, even when I tell them that some people call them mind maps, or spider diagrams; so I show them one of mine, for a topic they can follow, as an example of what I mean. They are also concerned about the use of 15 minutes of valuable time for something whose benefit they don't immediately see. So I make this as a suggestion just for the first tutorial, with my assurance that it will be of use to them and to me. But I promise that if they don't agree after this first try that it's worth while, we will abandon the reviewing in this way. (We have never decided not to continue!)

At the end of the tutorial time, I ask everyone to sit quietly for five minutes or so drawing their maps. Then I ask for a volunteer to share theirs. On the first occasion, this generally draws a blank, and ends up with me showing mine, because the students are reluctant to be the first to volunteer. But once mine is on the table, others quickly follow, telling or showing what is in their diagram – from interest in what *they* have and *I* haven't; or vice versa. As they compare and contrast their maps, they are each checking their understanding and coverage, and consolidating their learning at the same time, because the activity automatically builds in the review which is so valuable at this point. This also gives me the opportunity to do some instant remedial teaching, if there are clear gaps in understanding for most of the group, or to agree with them about what must go on the agenda for next time we meet.

This may also give me feedback for longer-term planning. For example, I realized from the concept maps this year that few of the students in the group had the familiarity with archaeological methods which I had (perhaps erroneously) depended on in previous years. They didn't readily understand site stratification, nor could they read a site map with ease. Consequently, as well as working with them immediately on these problems, I have also resolved to build in some early diagnostic work with next year's students, so that the pitch of what I plan will match their needs more accurately from the start.

This source of feedback can also provide some totally unexpected insights. For instance, John Cowan and I were once using it in the context of an introductory day for new Level 1 Open University students. We were running the morning session of the day school on 'being a student' for students across all faculties, and were going to hand over to faculty tutors for the afternoon.

One technology student, who had introduced himself as someone who had left school as early as he could, sat rather silently through the morning. Not long after taking part in the ice-breaking activity, he merged into the background, just looking into space and jotting occasional notes. We judged that we had utterly lost him. To our surprise, when everyone contributed their concept maps, David's consisted of a huge block in the centre of the page, emphasized with twiddles and double lines, which declared that he had suddenly understood – early in our session – what the first assignment was asking him to do. He had brought his lack of understanding as an intense worry to the day school, and the sheer relief of realization, from something that we had said early on, had just overwhelmed him, and made it possible for him to start thinking about what was being asked of him. What he had sat and done through most of the morning was just think through the implications for what he had been doing so far, and what he was going to do next. This was really valuable feedback to hand on to his course tutor, who could then respond to his concerns in specific detail. It was also reassuring information for John and myself; for the seemingly switched-off student was actually taking something highly useful from his participation in the tutorial – even if that had not been apparent to us, and was not quite what we expected or had planned for.

The most useful way to use the last part of a learning experience is to summarize what you have learnt in your own terms, to note omissions and inconsistencies, and to take immediate action accordingly, if that is at all possible. Unfortunately most learners, and most organized learning activities (which are often merely teaching presentations), are such that the time immediately after a learning experience is devoted to relaxing, or moving from one room to another, or seizing and consuming light refreshment. Making a brief time for concept mapping is one way of ensuring that a most important component of learning actually happens.

The nature of the method, in that it calls for a graphical response, tends to favour those with strong visual abilities, who can be at a disadvantage in verbal assignments. For that reason, you may wish to devote thought on how best to move such a learner on from the concept map to an explanatory statement or verbal explanation derived from it.

Another advantage and potential strength of concept mapping is that it can lead teacher and class into consideration of the topics covered, at greater depth than in the original activity, in order to complete the process of consolidation and clarify learning difficulties or inconsistencies.

It is highly likely that your students will quickly come to see mapping as a technique that is of use to them in learning and for other purposes. If they use it for summarizing and revising, then it has many strengths pedagogically. It impels assimilation in the learner's own words, it leads to the appreciation of structured relationships between components of learning, and it encourages the learner to concentrate on essentials, and to distinguish these from associated facts and ideas.

This is another good example of a method of formative evaluation which, once introduced, will become a natural part of the teacher's teaching strategy and from which formative evaluation data will then emerge almost incidentally, or as by-products.

A variant of this method, which does not depend on an ability to assemble thoughts in graphical form, is the 'focused list'. Each student is asked to write a word or phrase, chosen by the teacher, which sums up the learning on which the activity just completed should have concentrated. The teacher sets a time limit for the activity, or a limit on the number of items to be listed. Students then make a list of what they recall from the learning, in words or phrases. The tutor does the same and compares the intended list with the reality recorded on the student lists.

METHOD 5.2   PRE-TESTING AND POST-TESTING

Example

A lecturer in an engineering department produced some CAL materials that explained the origins and nature of the orthotropic behaviour of structural timber (the fact of having different properties in three orthogonal directions). He wanted to know if his learning materials were effective, and if so, how effective. So he constructed two tests, which he judged of comparable difficulty and equal validity in testing the learning he had defined in their outcomes.

He divided the class into two groups of matched ability, determined by their performance in a recent class examination. One group took test A before working with CAL and then test B; with the other group, the order of papers was reversed. So he was able to check the comparability of the tests, as well as measuring the learning.

The main findings were that:

- the tests were indeed comparable;
- few students had any relevant prior knowledge of the subject matter;
- all students scored well on their gain in factual recall;
- factual recall was rather better on the part of the poorer students (whose ability had been rated by performance in the previous class examination);
- low class scores on factual recall were associated with illustrations in the form of colour photographs, and not line diagrams;
- learning of the basic concepts was virtually nil;
- few students really understood orthotropicity.

The lecturer found this information a useful and formative input to the redesign of his materials.

Reservations about the approach described in this title have been expressed, for example, on the grounds that 'this is a paradigm for plants, not people'.[1] We would not be quite as critical, and offer you this approach as a reasonable way of finding out what students have learnt in a given activity, when it is possible to devise valid and reliable tests of the learning outcomes in question.

Note that a test that leads to marks or scores may not be necessary, or even appropriate. In some circumstances, it can be more suitable for the teacher to use a rating scale (eg for ability to use a theodolite) or a simple pass/fail check-list (eg for the ability to take a case history from a patient in hospital).[2]

Interpreting results

Pre- and post-test results should preferably be compared or analysed in terms of gain ratios, rather than the absolute value of the gain between one test and the other. A student who scored 40 per cent in the pre-test and 60 per cent in the post-test has registered an absolute gain of 20 per cent, as has a student whose pre-test score was 70 per cent and post-test 90 per cent. However, the former student has only gained 20 of the possible 60 marks between 40 and 100 – a gain ratio of $20/60 = 0.33$, whereas the second student has gained 20 of the 30 marks available, which is a gain ratio of $20/30 = 0.67$. In terms of gain ratios, the second is distinctly better than the first, and the gain ratio a more informative value through which to view the change.

METHOD 5.3   ANALYSIS OF EXAM ANSWERS

The previous methods were concerned with the determination of learning outcomes soon after the close of a learning activity. There is also some worth in scrutinizing learning outcomes at the end of a period of study, although these findings can be confounded by the effect of various variables.

Example

When I began work as a university teacher, I expected too much of my students, forgetting that they were learners and not the experienced graduates with whom I had been working in industry. My first examination paper was, therefore, far too demanding. When I produced my marks list, the acting head of department called me in and offered the succinct and wise advice that 'It's either your teaching or your examining – best decide which it is, and do something about it'.

That advice led me to be continually cautious about what was revealed about my teaching – or my examining – in my students' examination performances. And so it has been that I have always returned to the examination scripts after examining the students, and have proceeded to examine myself. I summarize the choice students have made of questions (even where options are *not* offered, there is the option to have no time to do some questions!), and I ask myself why some questions, and topics, were unpopular. I summarize the marks scored in each question, when attempted, and I ask myself why some marks were low and some quite high. I summarize the weaknesses that led to loss of marks, and ask myself why some are fairly common across the class group – and what I should be doing about that. Such analysis is an informative contribution to my formative evaluation of my work.

We feel that this says it all, although we would also refer you to Chapter 8 for further thoughts on the formative evaluation of assessment to which this example is linked.

METHOD 5.4   RSQC2

One of the most common techniques for use shortly after a class experience is to ask the students to focus quickly on their learning – to their advantage needless to say!

Either at the end of the class or at the beginning of the next one (an important distinction) you can ask students to make notes of what they can recall of the learning. Once they have had, say, a couple of minutes to do this, you should ask them to pick out up to five main points which they are then to rank in order of importance. This is the R of the title – *recall*.

Next, in what may be a difficult exercise first time round, get them to summarize as many of their important points as possible in one sentence, which should be a suitable summary of what was at the heart of the learning in that class. This is the S – *summary*.

Next, get them to write down one or perhaps two questions, which they felt were left unanswered, for them, at the close of the class – *question*.

After that, they should try to *connect*, the first of the two Cs, what was learnt in this class to the content of the module or course, as a whole. And finally, for the second C, they should *comment* evaluatively on what they found worth while or negative in their experience of that class.

You should collect that feedback, and indicate how you will summarize it, act upon what emerges from it, and report back.

This method will provide immediate feedback about what was recalled of the learning, what questions remain and should presumably receive your attention, and how the students relate this class to the course as a whole. However, it can be time-consuming, as 2–3 minutes will be required for each stage. It can also submerge you in data that you cannot possibly analyse.

Summary

- The most suitable way to find out about progress towards learning outcomes is to use a valid and reliable test, before and after an activity, to provide that information.
- Valid and reliable tests being hard to come by, and time-consuming in use; a reasonable alternative is to get the students to rehearse their learning (which is itself a sound pedagogical practice), and to confirm its adequacy.
- Examinations held some time after a teaching and learning activity measure learning confounded by other activities – including remedial work.[3]

Notes

1. See Parlett, M and Hamilton, D (1972) *Evaluation as Illumination: A new approach to the study of innovatory programmes*, University of Edinburgh, Centre for Research in Educational Sciences. This, perhaps the most quoted reference in the field of evaluation, was one of the several writings in which the status quo in evaluation at that time was vigorously criticized, and a viable alternative offered.
2. See, as an example of this methodology (which began in the Centre for Medical Education in the University of Dundee, with the work of Professor R McG Harden), the Objective Structured Clinical Examinations. This had considerable impact on testing for medical education and subjects allied to medicine. The method is rather like circuit training and involves demonstration of components of skills with a rigorous method of observing and assessing. See Hounsell, D, McCulloch, M and Scott, M (eds) (1996) *The ASSHE Inventory*, Centre for Teaching, Learning and Assessment, University of Edinburgh, and Napier University.
3. There is a perhaps apocryphal tale of a lecture so bad that it inspired frantic library work, and led to exemplary examination scores. Apocryphal or not, the point is still valid that many possible factors confound the teaching given in formal classes and tested some time later.

CHAPTER 6

Obtaining information about student reactions after the experience

We emphasize that, in this chapter and as the heading implies, both the obtaining and the reactions take place *'after* the experience'. For that reason they must inevitably include a measure of opinion tempered by mellowing, or the effects of frequent replay, rather than an exclusive concentration on hard facts – and so they should be interpreted and used accordingly.

METHOD 6.1   QUESTIONNAIRES

This title covers a wide-ranging class of methods, rather than simply being another of the options open to you. This section should be read with that point in mind.

The comments which follow outline significant points about a methodology on which there is a substantial literature[1] which you should certainly consult before engaging in the design of questionnaires. It is advisable, for example, to use questionnaires that are short and simple, and to do so only occasionally, for example at the end of a course or after some important learning experience. It is also important to consider, before asking a question, what we would do with the various possible answers. If there is no obvious use for the answer, then the question surely needs to be changed or omitted.

It is worth noting that students sometimes have fears about the recognition of their handwriting on a questionnaire return (a point which relates to other written methods of evaluation as well, although nowadays word processors can be readily employed). If any of your students are unconvinced by your reassurances that you are genuinely seeking data on which to review and improve – for *their* benefit, and without needing to know from whom particular responses originated – then the simple suggestion could be made to a class that those so concerned get someone else to fill in that part of the form on their behalf.

Forms of question

The concept of the 'questionnaire' encompasses a great variety of possibilities. It goes almost without saying that all involve questions, answers and responses – the questions being asked by or on behalf of the evaluator; the answers usually being provided by students, although a few questionnaires are directed to teachers; and the responses being the aspect of the method which (interestingly) receive least attention in the literature.

For obvious reasons, the questions should be:

- short, and deal with a single point;
- clear, comprehensible, and lacking in jargon and ambiguity;
- such that they do not lead to an expected answer;
- capable of being answered independently of other questions;
- free from ambiguous or vague words;
- written in a positive form (since negative forms can confuse);
- free from questioner's bias.

Questions can be asked either in an open-ended format or as closed questions, or as a mixture of the two. Closed questions ask for a specific answer – a circle round an option, items to be ranked, and so on. Open-ended questions allow students to express their view, either in a single word or in a fuller statement. Any pattern of questioning, of course, can be supplemented by leaving space for 'any other comments?' which allows students to add views that are not pre-ordained by the tutor's range of questions.

The questions can thus be of two main forms. The popular option, presumably chosen for cost-effective processing or anonymity or both, is to link a question to a choice of predetermined answers. This will inevitably determine the focus of both question and answer, even if the possible answers are set (as is customary) on some graded scale which ranges from one statement or description to another. The simple 'Yes/No', or other binary option, is less popular because it offers less choice and less detail of feedback in response, but that reservation then equally opens to question the choice and detail of the responses to other closed questions.

The closed-answer form certainly ensures anonymity, and leads to a speedy completion of the questionnaire, but this exercise can degenerate into filling in an aptly named 'happiness sheet'. Admittedly, in minor variants of the closed-ended question approach, respondents may be invited to add comments *if they so wish*, or they may be asked to give explanations of their choices. The latter possibility is worth considering, because it focuses on the thinking behind the answer, and can enrich the quality of feedback information in both closed-*and* open-ended question forms. Open-ended questionnaires can thus be regarded as semi-structured, in that they are specific in indicating the topics on which they are seeking feedback, but make no assumptions about what that feedback might be.

Likert-type[2] scales (with responses from 1–5 agreeing or disagreeing in varying strengths with the statements positioned at each end of the range) are useful for assessing a student's attitude between strongly disagree, disagree, neither agree nor disagree, agree and strongly agree. To avoid a run of unthinking responses on one end of the scale or the other, it is desirable to vary positive with negative statements – pointing out to the unwary that you have done this. However, such scales will suffer from the possibility that each respondent attaches different shades of meaning to the qualifying adverbs[3] and even that the respondents will view the descriptors as being located at the same intervals on a scale. The amalgamation of results from such questionnaires must, therefore, be viewed with that caution in mind. By contrast, the professional questionnaire designer might set out to produce a Thurstone Scale questionnaire,[4] a much more arduous task that attempts to obtain information on attitudes using a scale that should offer genuinely equal intervals. But this is surely a task only for those who specialize in questionnaire design, and beyond the scope of this guide.

Questionnaires using fixed answers are certainly useful to specialist units engaged in undertaking evaluations for courses with large numbers of students. The method enables results to be obtained relatively quickly and cheaply, and to be presented reliably in easily assimilated forms. However, the instruments *do* need to be competently designed, since poor questions can lead to findings of dubious validity, and can present time-consuming problems of analysis. In large numbers, questionnaires call for access to a data-handling facility, but above all, for our current purposes, they reveal relatively little about the quality of the learning experience and process, and offer few insights into the nature of possible improvements in teaching – and in learning.

Badly designed questions will lead to poor or misleading information. For example, an evaluation of an Open University course asked students to rate the various components of the course, including the resource materials. One item to be rated was 'the audio tapes'. This created difficulties for thoughtful student respondents, for the general verdict was that two of the six tapes were excellent, two were reasonable and two were dreadful. What answer should be given in such circumstances, and how well informed is the evaluator, and the course leader, when receiving this blanket response?

Open-ended questions are costly in time to analyse and interpret, and yield findings which are difficult to analyse and lengthy to report. However, if the sampling is careful and the analysis sufficiently rigorous to promise reliability, they offer the great advantages of allowing students to explain, to raise issues and to qualify their responses; they generate persuasive and illuminating quotations which stimulate pedagogic discussion and action; and consequently, they are more likely to inform revisions which are appropriate and effective.[5] Overall, we imagine that you will leave closed-ended questionnaires to your institution, although you will want to read and reflect on their findings; but you will probably find good use in your own formative evaluation for open-ended questions or questionnaires.

Choosing the subject matter

When enquiring into the quality of the students' learning experience, you should be acutely aware that it is important to ensure that questionnaire enquiries consider *all* possible contributory factors, rather than just those that involve teachers. Library and other sources of resource, for example, are often neglected, and even when they are remembered, the librarians and their activities are usually still omitted from the circulation list for the feedback which has been sought.[6]

It is also important in questionnaire design, as in all formative evaluation, to be as assiduous in seeking to identify good practice which should be retained and consolidated, as to pinpoint the weaknesses which need to be eliminated. This principle should be borne in mind when you choose topics for questions, and when you frame the questions.

Question form is the most familiar aspect of questionnaire design to be debated; but it is surely more important to consider carefully the options open to the evaluator, or evaluative teacher, in arriving at the critical choice of subject matter for the questions. The right choice can be determined in a wide number of ways:

- The teacher or evaluator can simply use a standard institutional questionnaire form, or a form that has been widely used elsewhere.

This avoids the perils attendant on amateur design of a survey instrument, but suffers from the limitations of applying a general enquiry to a particular situation.

- The class group, or the class committee, may generate their own headings and question forms for the questionnaire, through some facilitating framework of group work.
- The topics to be covered may be chosen in view of the issues raised during a small series of pilot interviews with students, seeking suggestions about matters on which feedback should be obtained. Topics may also emerge from other methods of enquiry, such as concept maps or IPR.
- The questions (for an open-ended enquiry) may be chosen to allow students freedom to provide feedback on the matters of most importance to them. A useful example of this is the simple request from the teacher to be told what teacher and course team should *stop* doing next year, what they should *continue* to do, and what they should *start* to do, which they haven't done this year.[7]
- The teacher and colleagues may well already have good reason to include certain issues in the questionnaire, since they have clearly been or are difficulties for the students, or are successful and should be confirmed as such.

Example

Interviews can be used to lay the groundwork for a questionnaire. I was planning to send a questionnaire out to all students in one particular catchment area of the OU to find out their reactions to the Learning Skills programme which had recently been run there. My concern was that if I simply designed the questionnaire myself, the questions asked would be the ones I would articulate from my own particular point of view. But what I also, or even mainly, wanted to find out was student views on the issues that *they* found significant. So I asked for a dozen student volunteers to spend a couple of hours having a glass of wine and nibbles, and to help me by brainstorming what they saw as questions which should be raised. I explained the purpose of the session, settled them into two groups, each with a tutor (myself and a colleague) to act as facilitator and clerk, and I asked them to flip-chart issues which they saw as significant, and which they thought it important to get student views on. The resulting sheets covered much the same ground as I would have considered, but there were important differences of emphasis, and one or two items, important to the students, which would not have occurred to me.

Interviews can be a useful means of gaining insight into students' learning, but usually only in conjunction with other methods. On their own, though, they risk being unrepresentative and not rigorous.

Example

We recently streamlined the planning of tutorial provision for OU students in Scotland, concentrating tutorials in the larger centres, and providing fewer, but longer, tutorial sessions. This was a considerable change for students, for tutors, and for the senior academics and administrators. The small steering group wanted to get as much feedback as possible from everyone concerned before the next planning round, but we wanted to avoid prejudging the impact the changes might have had by even determining the areas on which we would ask questions in a questionnaire. So we conducted a number of telephone interviews, on a structured list of open-ended questions, to enable us to shape the questionnaire. On the basis of the responses, we rejected entirely some questions we had been thinking of asking – students simply did not perceive as an issue the safety aspects of the campus or the building they attended; but we added in others – we realized that we needed to ask for, and use, more detail, for example, about the distances students had travelled to attend.

Obtaining responses

Obtaining adequate responses is a vexed issue when questionnaire enquiries are conducted. Often the returns are from such a small, and not necessarily representative, section of the class that there must be grave doubts about the information that they provide. High rates of return, however, normally come from situations in which an immediate response is arranged, with consequent loss of opportunity for reflection on the part of the students.

In seeking response, you, or the evaluator, may:

- hand out forms in class, give time for responses to be completed and then collect in the forms from all the students who are present. This could present difficulties for those students who want time to reflect on their experience of the class or course, and to provide a full and considered response;
- hand out the forms, ask for a full response, provide a simple method of return and then wait. This can give more security for anonymous responses, and more time for consideration, but it may lead to very low response rates;

- declare a small number of questions in class on an overhead projector, ask for responses there and then, and get the students to drop slips of paper with numbered answers into a box as they leave. This provides speedy and anonymous feedback on questions whose answers matter to you, and on which you can and will act speedily;
- display the questions on a flip-chart sheet in informal classes like labs and small group activities, and arrange for students to add their votes, in five-bar stroke gates, during class. This has the advantage that the results are known to the students almost immediately, and you and they may engage in discussion of what to do about them, before the class disperses;
- computerize questions and responses, provided the use of the computer does not deter respondents. This approach can then be coupled to computerized analysis of responses.

Analysis

In analysing the responses to closed questions, you should at least sum up, and bear in mind subsequently:

- the number of students who responded to each question;
- the proportion of students in the class who provided each response;
- the frequency of responses for each possibility;
- the mean or average score for each question;
- an indication of the type of distribution – tight or spread, balanced or skew;
- cross-tabulations for different sub-groups within the sample, by gender, ability or experience.

Similarly, for open-ended questions, you should:

- work with individual comments, in a physical or electronic scissors-and-paste activity;
- provisionally group the comments by the topic to which they refer;
- on a second pass, and having attempted to use the first set of headings, be prepared to revise and refine to get appropriate precision and suitable coverage;
- précis where that is meaningful, but otherwise list comments verbatim.

Types of feedback

To describe the types of feedback that you may have to handle, we offer these categories, in italics, following some specific examples of feedback from mainly recent questionnaire evaluations. These examples are genuine, but, we hasten to add, did not all come from the one class or institution.

You could find yourself handling such feedback as:

- 'Jim's tutorials are great. He is a fun person, and makes us feel at home. It's good to get to know some of the others in the class in this way, early on'. *(Praise for the event, which tells you nothing about the learning or even your teaching.)*
- 'It's an insult. The classrooms are old-fashioned and dirty, and the library is always overcrowded and short of the key texts'. *(Expression of anger, or of resentment.)*
- 'You often get too near the overhead projector, and black out the words on the screen'. *(Useful information about something that is not going well, and can be rectified.)*
- 'I strongly dislike the way you cover up your transparencies on the OHP and only let us see the words when it suits you; why don't you let us see everything from the start?' *(Critical comment from about 40 per cent of the class with no strong view from the rest – class preferences.)*
- The personal feedback to a lecturer whose module was rated the best of six under various headings that she was (in various responses) 'not well ordered, gave unclear explanations, and rushed the learners over-much'. This was in an institutional questionnaire where the favourable responses had been on the left, until the questions about individual lecturers – where the order was reversed. Presumably students had got into the habit of expressing favour on the left-hand side of the range of offered options. *(Questionable responses.)*
- On an overseas postgraduate course, with high fees: 'The so-called summer school week didn't do any of the things promised in the programme, and was simply devoted to course evaluation and explaining the regulations which were so unclear in the booklet'. *(Information of which senior management had hitherto been unaware.)*
- On a course encouraging critical thinking: 'He doesn't tell us what he wants us to know, but leaves us to work that out for ourselves'. (This feedback, incidentally, was presented as a criticism, but was taken by the tutor concerned as praise!) *(A lack of perception by students of intended outcomes and actual learning.)*
- An average rating of 2.3 for one module in a programme – on a scale where 5 is most positive – and where other modules rate 3.8–4.3.

Something is going wrong – but what? And, in the same survey, a module rating of 4.1 with responses in the range 3–5; and another also rating 4.1, but with more responses of 5 than of 4, and a few at 1. What is troubling the minority in the second case? *(Indirect messages to prompt a reflective enquiry.)*

Notice, or deduce, that the most useful feedback came from open-ended questions or volunteered comment, that the vague and unhelpful responses probably came from questions which were too general, and that some of the important feedback from closed-ended questions, with rating on a five-point scale, called for further investigation – once it had been properly analysed and considered.

In using questionnaires, beware of their overuse, or similarly excessive length. Students can rapidly become resistant and the exercise may be counter-productive. So take care not to create this reaction to no good purpose.

You should always test your plan and design against the 'So what?' question. If you are not going to be able to make good use of any or all of the information you ingather, abandon the idea. There is nothing worse than drowning in a sea of detailed responses only to suddenly realize that you don't know what you are going to do with them. So take care to ensure that the length *and detail* of the questionnaire is suitable for your purpose. If you just want to find out whether the activity was useful and generally welcome, a simple 'happiness sheet' will suffice. If you are interested in eliciting a more complex quantity and quality of information, it may be as well to consult some of the specialist literature, or ask a professional about the design of your form, or use another method. It can often be more useful to compile a short and relevant questionnaire by listing perhaps five specific questions whose answers you really want to know and will use, and formulating appropriate coded responses on a five-point scale.

Finally, if you have to analyse data from a large-scale enquiry, think ahead to the software you may wish to use where you need to look at correlations, for example, between fields of data.

METHOD 6.2   INTERVIEWS[8]

Enquiring conversations with students, of varying degrees of formality, can all be a form of interview. An exchange with a student with whom you are on easy terms can give you the opportunity to ask a question or two about their experience of your classes, and what they are finding helpful. A slightly more formal version might be by prior arrangement with a few of your class, allowing you to focus on selected points, but not constraining them from elaborating as they feel fit. The most structured version would tie you, or an enquirer on your behalf, to a declared set of questions – often quite brief and not very open-ended. In this latter option, you mainly obtain information on specific matters, provided without much deep thought or feeling.

When receiving feedback in person, listen carefully. Wait until later to ask questions about anything that puzzled you, and then only ask for the data that supports or amplifies the assertions made. Note the useful technique (provided it is not used in a manner perceived as threatening) of asking 'Why?' repeatedly – to find out the assumptions and principles which underlie a description of aims or actions. Similarly, it can often help gain access to a rich seam of information if you ask 'Can you give me an example of that?'

Example   The informal, conversational, interview

I walked round to the pub after the OU tutorial with one of my students. We had already got to know each other through a series of phone calls she had made earlier about work problems, in the course of which we had shared experiences about the difficulties of juggling work and family commitments. I had been wondering how well the decision to focus just on the *Iliad* during this session had worked, and whether the students would have found it helpful at this stage to start explicitly linking the heroic values expressed in this poem with those of the *Odyssey*. Her strong preference for the latter made me check it out with the other students in the pub as the agenda for our next tutorial, 'unless anyone really feels they want to spend more time just on the *Iliad*', saving time and creating instant momentum in the right direction by that touch of informal feedback, which led into the possibility of succinct and meaningful communication with the entire group.

More formally I might have offered the options for discussion within the class, asking the students generally to report on how they were getting on and what would suit them best. Or, more formally still, if I had thought that far ahead, I could have given them a short set of diagnostic questions at the end of the previous tutorial, just to test the water and check for progress – and then planned accordingly.

The mention in the next example of unobtrusive note taking is worthy of comment. For in any interview situation, note taking is a challenge. In face-to-face situations, it may inhibit both interviewer and interviewee, and can certainly limit eye contact. Even on the telephone, it takes time, may not be accurate once transcribed and influences the process of the interview.

Example   A structured interview

I worked with a colleague who was, like me, interested to learn what students took from our tutorials, and what it was that we did in our tuition which helped, and perhaps disappointed, them. We agreed to work as a pair, and pinpointed first of all the topics on which we should seek information. These headings were – successes, disappointments, effective actions on our parts and ineffective ones.

We each approached three of our students, and asked them to assist. We explained that they would take part in the teaching and learning activities as usual, but that we would give them a note beforehand of the questions that our colleague would be asking them about – after the event. We set out our four questions on a handout, and encouraged the students to have them in mind during the activity, and to make rough notes, for their own purposes, immediately after the event and before our colleague contacted them. Our questions were:

1. What were the most important learning outcomes for you in this activity? (Up to three.)

2. What were the most important disappointments for you, in that you didn't learn or understand something that you had hoped to make progress with? (Up to three.)

3. What things did the tutor do which made the activity particularly effective for you – and why were these helpful? (Up to three.)

4. What, if anything, did the tutor do which you found unhelpful? (Up to three.)

Immediately after the event, I contacted my colleague's students, one by one. In this case, I did so by telephone. I had purposefully not discussed the content of the activity with my colleague, nor had she told me what learning outcomes she hoped to achieve. We felt that that was an advantage as it precluded any leading questions from the enquirer to the students. I posed the questions, one by one, as they were set out on the handout. After I had listened carefully to an answer, I asked questions of clarification or amplification, so that I could give a full report to my colleague. But I introduced nothing new in my supplementary questioning, relating it to what I had been told in the first answer. Using the telephone, I was able to make notes unobtrusively. When I had finished my questions, I summarized what I had been told with the aid of these notes, and checked all of this with the student. Then I reported back to my colleague, without relating any particular response to a named student. Sometimes my colleague would check a response or reaction with the complete class.

Some habits and dodges that are worth cultivating or using are to:

- Develop your own 'curtailed word' shorthand.
- Use a list of *possible* questions, ring the ones you use, and note the responses alongside them.
- Make time in your schedule to expand notes immediately after the interview while the messages are still accessible for recall.
- Use an audio-recording, not so much to play back and/or transcribe (which takes an age) but to check points in your notes of which you are unsure.
- Use a video-recording, to pick up body language.
- Even without a video-recording, make notes of body language, rapid eye movement, pauses and so on.
- Talk back your most important points to the interviewee, check them for accuracy and comprehensiveness, and note anything said to you thereafter as part of the interview – for interviewees *can* have second thoughts!
- Take extreme care, even to the extent of getting someone else to check through, about the danger of bias in selecting what to note, and in your abstracting.[9]

METHOD 6.3   DELPHI TECHNIQUES

This is a fairly simple approach, enabling you to obtain a composite version of the responses from a complete group of students, thoughtfully and without rushing the respondents.

Example

A group of students had taken part in a series of learning skills workshops, which were of an innovatory format and had involved staff who had not taken part in any such venture before. It was important to us, therefore, to find out from the students what they felt – in retrospect – had been the strengths and weaknesses of the workshops, and what changes they felt we might make to improve them for the next group of students. We wanted the students to reflect on their experience, and to give us thoughtful and considered advice – and not to be deterred from so doing by the fear that their own particular personal contribution would be identifiable.

We went through the following sequence of consultation using an enquirer who had not been a member of the teaching team:

1. The enquirer asked students individually and in their separate locations to note down what they felt had been the strengths and weaknesses of the workshops, and what advice they would give us for the next iteration of the series.

2. She then analysed all the contributions, and drew up a composite summary of the workshops on that basis.

3. This summary was then given to each individual student to read through on his or her own. The students asked to suggest changes, to note any omissions and to correct any inaccuracies.

4. The summary was then revised.

5. The revision was returned for further suggestions – a process that could have been repeated had we felt there was still comment to be elicited.

This timescale, and the anonymity of this method, ensured a comprehensive coverage of individual views; it avoided the dominant influence of outspoken participants; and it gave the students time for careful and considered thought. At the same time, however, it required commitment and time from them. The feedback we obtained was detailed, soundly based and constructive.

METHOD 6.4   A LETTER TO NEXT YEAR'S STUDENTS

Example

While on academic audit business, I encountered a department of health care that had an interesting story to tell about their method of obtaining data to inform their regular process of annual course review.

A lecturer would explain to the students in class that she wanted them to write a letter of advice to next year's students. The letter should tell them about the attractions and the less attractive parts of the course, and about what mattered most in it; it should also suggest how best to approach effective study. Generally, it should tell the newcomers as much as possible of what they, the present year's students, wished someone had told *them* before they started.

The lecturer arranged how this task would be tackled, and took her class through the plan. Then she helped them to work through the first steps she had described. First, she asked each student to take five minutes or so to reflect, privately, and to jot down (in their own shorthand) points that they would wish the letter to mention. Then she arranged for the students to get together in quartets, and come up with a composite list. In this way, any controversial points were helpfully anonymized for – other than within the quartet – no one knew who had originated them.

Finally the lecturer recruited two volunteers to be clerk and chair for the full class plenary which followed. Reminding them about what to do next, she then withdrew. The chair began by seeking suggestions and agreement from the plenary group about what the letter should and should not contain; as this proceeded, the clerk maintained a visible record, on the whiteboard.

The chair then asked for two or three students to help the clerk to draft and edit the letter. Once the drafting group had produced their letter, it was posted on the noticeboard for class comment, revised accordingly and then passed on to the lecturer.

The lecturer used the letter, as she had indicated from the outset, in two ways. She gave it without comment, though with an indication of its source, to the incoming students in the following year; and she abstracted from it (for her action) any points that she felt called for her attention before or during the following year.

In the example quoted to me, the lecturer identified, for example, the need for a justification of one topic whose relevance had not been established for this class group, leaving the students bewildered by, and without motivation for, that topic. She found a general desire for *examples* of the type of case study she required of the students in their coursework, rather than the mere description of what a good case study would feature (which was what she had given them up till then). And she learnt the real importance of the social gathering which she had arranged at the beginning of the year to let members of an assorted group come to know each other; clearly the most important outcome for the students had been the relief of discovering that others shared their (eventually unfounded) fears about the demands of the course.

This form of evaluation seemed a useful notion to me. At the time I encountered it, I was teaching an OU course, with limited class contact time; and I had a class group of which only a few could attend face-to-face tutorials. The method clearly would not transfer without some modifications.

I told the students (by telephone) about the example I have just described, and asked if they would like to help me by each writing an individual letter to next year's students – and, like the other tutor, I promised to use some of these. I provided no prompting, nor did I offer suggestions about the form that the letters should take. I made it clear that I would also analyse the messages that I found within the letters, and would do what I could to respond to the points where a response was within my power. I undertook to provide each letter writer with my summary of the messages that I found within the letters as a whole, and of my intended responses.

> Of the main points which emerged, two led to informed action, one called for no action but was welcome reinforcement of a message that I, the tutor, had already tried to convey; and one told me that a practice on which I set store, but about which I was doubtful, appeared in the eyes of my students to be effective.

It only takes simple preparation to obtain this feedback, and there is a relatively slight workload from the analysis and summary. It provides indirect and reasonably authentic insight, mainly about the nature of learning difficulties with both the course and the tuition, as perceived by the students. Comments can give heartening and constructive insight into how and why students react well to aspects of your teaching style and planning.

The feedback, especially if accumulated over a year or so, can provide you with a substantial bank of useful advice for every new group of students, all the better because it will be worded in the kind of language which conveys a lot, since another student wrote it.

In a variant, the class – or individuals, for that matter – can be asked to write a letter which can be suitably anonymized (especially electronically) to make suggestions to the tutor about how to approach the following year. Although this might seem simply a different way of asking for 'stop/start/continue' feedback, the context of the enquiry tends to lead to more frank and meaningful consideration – and hence feedback.

In yet another variant, students can be asked to write to their tutor *before* beginning their studies, declaring their expectations and their reasons for taking a particular module. This can reveal a great deal about expectations and motivation which may be a surprise to the tutor – and hence a valuable source of guidance.

METHOD 6.5 A CLOSING 'WASH-UP' SESSION – PERHAPS WITH A PREPARATORY SESSION

At the end of a module, or a run of tutorials or workshops, you can readily schedule time to step aside and review progress with your students. You can prepare for this by having had a matching session at the start of the series when you together explore expectations and objectives.

Example

As a student a few years ago at Alverno College in Milwaukee, I took part in the first session of the course on 'American Women in the Civil War'. We all had copies of the course syllabus, which detailed clearly the course objectives, both in terms of the source material and content to be covered, and also in terms of the kind of development as learners it was expected that the course would help us to make. Alverno College assessment focuses not just on the acquisition of knowledge, but centrally on the competencies with which the student works on that knowledge – handling values, analysing, communicating and so on. So this first session of four hours gave us students the opportunity to work in small groups and go through the course outline, working out for ourselves what the path ahead was going to look like from our individual starting points, reaching an understanding of what the college expected of us, and having the chance to add to the formal course objectives any extra ones we might have ourselves. A fellow student, for example, set a marker for the fact that she would like to add for herself the objective of tracking down her great-grandmother's history during this period, an objective she was encouraged to add, provided that she also worked out how she would demonstrate that she had achieved it.

Expectations and aspirations were thoroughly explored. The matching wash-up sessions, perhaps in mid-course, but certainly at the end, would similarly review the match between where the students had started and where they had finished.

What can be achieved in such 'time out' depends greatly on how sophisticated the students are as learners. If they are relatively unaware of the process and are not in the habit of reflecting critically on their own progress as learners, the outcomes will be mainly in terms of content coverage. If, like Alverno learners, they are thoughtful self-assessors, the insights into learning development and growth can be deep and dynamic; the whole session can transform the individual's perception of his or her own development into a jointly owned analysis of what the group processes have created.

METHOD 6.6   'NOT QUITE' ROUNDS

Here, students may speak to a particular question or a theme on which you want feedback – perhaps the effectiveness of arrangements for access to required reading material in the library, or the pacing of a tutorial on a difficult topic. Participants speak in any order, but only if they so wish. There is no pressure to contribute, and a student can just say 'pass', or nothing at all. It helps if the suggestion is made that no one speaks a second time until the others seem to have dried up – and if a mild suggestion is made that no one speaks for more than, say, three minutes. Responses are unobtrusively recorded (usually by a colleague who acts as clerk), and are later summarized, and displayed at some convenient point, after which students can offer written postscript comments to be added to the record.

The method, as we have suggested here, had its origins in the evaluation of international staff development activities on Research and Creative Teaching, run by the Swedish National Board for Higher Education. There, it had the useful characteristic that the tone of the contributions tended to ebb and flow. A series of positive comments might then provoke some 'Ah, yes, but ...' contributions; and a series of criticisms had a similar effect in bringing out some of the positives. This refinement on the straight 'round', in which each student in turn comments or passes, is worth trying out.

METHOD 6.7   COLLECTING POST-ITS

In an approach similar to the previous one, students can be asked to write their comments on a question or issue on Post-its. They then stick the Post-its up on a board or wall, perhaps under appropriate headings, adding any further comments which occur to them when they see the others. You summarize, and then display your summary of the responses.

A helpful pair of questions to suggest is:

'What was the most important learning for you in this class activity?'

'What important question remains unanswered for you at the end of this class?'

Alternatively, particularly if you are a pessimist, you may wish to use:

'What was the most obscure part of the class for you?'

This is a useful approach to allow students to blow off steam immediately after an event, and while still fresh from it. It also allows them to provide quick and full feedback, which may identify significant points that you wish to follow up with other evaluative techniques or changes you wish to put in place immediately. However, remember that the summaries may not cover the views of all the students, and may well reflect reactions at one particular part of the programme, concentrating on current ups and downs.

METHOD 6.8   FOCUS GROUPS

A focus group is another useful technique to use when you have identified a question or issue you would like to explore with a group of students and now want to discover their feelings and opinions about the given problem, experience or other matter.

Example

We had sent out a questionnaire to all participants asking their views on a range of matters, mainly concerning practicalities which seemed relevant to us. One of us worked systematically and compiled an analysis of responses under various headings. As we were formulating recommendations on major curricular issues, we felt that we needed to explore whether our understanding of the concerns expressed through the questionnaires was accurate, and whether there were other aspects of issues to be taken into account.

We invited a small group of eight participants to come to a meeting, which was preceded by a sandwich lunch (some of these people had travelled considerable distances) and was advertised as lasting no more than three hours. The facilitator had defined the broad themes from the questionnaires, and took the group through these, allowing them space to reflect on and elaborate the formulation of issues. He unobtrusively flip-charted responses, and circled back to these at the end, explicitly checking with the group that this was a fair and accurate record of the points they wished to make. The flip-chart record was then a basis for the report, which was subsequently written up, and, after discussion by the team, translated into recommendations.

Such focus group work can be used to:

- identify and confirm key issues;
- develop emerging themes or concerns;
- articulate concerns or generate hypotheses;
- expand and illuminate quantitative feedback;
- develop courses or student support in a learner-directed way;
- get feedback on interim interpretations of findings from other sources.

The method works best with small groups, of between 6 and 12 students, who represent the constituency whose views you wish to elicit. If your purpose is the exploration of general themes, you can let the conversation flow, just steering it gently to ensure that all the themes are covered. However, if you have a more formal and precisely identified programme of points to cover, you may need to timekeep more carefully, and be more directive in your steering of the discussion.

You need to think carefully about how you are to record the points arising from the discussion. Sometimes it may be appropriate to build in a flip-chart record as in the example we have described. However you may wish to consider having an unobtrusive clerk, sitting at the back of the class and noting any apparently significant comments, which can then be checked back with the group at the end; or you may wish to audio- or video-record, though the transcription and/or later analysis of data from either of these puts considerable additional demands on your time.

It is also important to have decided in advance on the level of analysis you are aiming for. You may wish for qualitative analysis, a systematic content clustering, or a more 'ethnographic' approach – or a combination of these.[10]

METHOD 6.9   STOP/START/CONTINUE

Example

At the end of the first semester of our course, we arranged for the students to take part in a number of open-ended activities designed to provide us with data for formative evaluation. In one of these, starting from the snowballing of individual responses, the student chair got the group to assemble a list of advice or requests to the course team under three headings.

One of these was that we should 'stop' doing some things that we were doing, which the students found unhelpful. They were asked to tell us why this was so. Similarly, they were asked to list items under the heading 'start', where they listed things that we might do, but hadn't been doing so far, which they would find useful; and again they explained why they were making this request. Finally they told us to 'continue' doing some of the things we had been doing, which they found useful, because...'.

Three things need to be said about this data. First, we judge that it was important that the students knew that we genuinely wanted to know not just what we had been getting right, but what we had been getting wrong, or had omitted. Second, the data was extremely useful, and informed several significant changes in the module design and delivery before the next cohort arrived. And, finally, some of the data was surprising, and was on matters that would not have figured had we built up a feedback questionnaire.

Stop/start/continue can be used in many situations and forms; it makes sense to students; and it can yield rich data, collated and assembled by the student group.

Summary

We reiterate the caution in our opening to this chapter. The methods we have described here depend on the memories of students and participants in your programmes, for they are used some time after the event. We are well aware of the factors which are relevant in other circumstances, when memories fade, are replayed and distorted, or otherwise prove unreliable. All these apply here too. You will find the methods we have described thought-provoking and a source of potentially rich insights. However, these outcomes then need to be checked.

Notes

1. See Robson, C (1993) *Real World Research: A resource for social scientists and practitioner-researchers*, pp 227–68, Blackwell, Oxford, and especially the Further Reading section on pp 267–68. Or, on a scale appropriate to formative evaluations, Munn, P and Drever, E (1990) *Using Questionnaires in Small-scale Research,* Scottish Council for Research in Education, Edinburgh. Or, an earlier and well-tried volume, Oppenheim, A N (1966) *Questionnaire Design and Attitude Measurement*, Heinemann, London. And, with an emphasis on evaluation for the practitioner, Thorpe, M (1988) *Evaluating Open and Distance Learning*, Longman, Harlow.
2. For further discussion of various scales and tests, including Likert, Thurstone and Guttman scales, see Robson, C (1993) *Real World Research: A resource for social scientists and practitioner-researchers*, Blackwell, Oxford.
3. Low, G (1995) 'Hallelujah, very': responding to 'very' in questionnaire items, *Evaluation and Research in Education*, **9** (1), pp 15–28.
4. See Note 2 above.
5. See Chambers, E (1992) Improving foundation level study at the Open University through evaluation of the student experience, in *Proceedings of the CNAA Conference on 'Evaluating the quality of the student experience'*, Council for National Academic Awards, London
6. O'Shea, arguing that students must play a greater role in defining and formulating the quality of the education which they experience, describes how part of that challenge was tackled by a mixture of diary-keeping, tracking, telephone survey, group feedback and a questionnaire; see O'Shea, T (1992) Evaluating the educational experience of student, *Proceedings of the CNAA Conference on 'Evaluating the quality of the student experience'*, London. Cf Revil, D reporting a complementary approach to the same challenge at the same conference, in Student experience of higher education and the role of libraries.
7. See Method 6.9, page 90.

8. For further guidance on interviewing, see Robson, C (1993) *Real World Research: A resource for social scientists and practitioner-researchers*, pp 227–68, Blackwell, Oxford.

9. See also the comments on recording in Method 3.3, page 40.

10. For more detail of use of this approach, see, eg Basch, C E (1987) Focus group interview: an under-utilised research technique for improving theory and practice in health education, *Health Education Quarterly*, **14**, pp 411–48. For valuable comment on the analysis of data generally, see Robson, C (1993) *Real World Research: A resource for social scientists and practitioner-researchers*, Blackwell, Oxford, pp 303–408.

CHAPTER 7

IDENTIFYING TOPICS THAT MERIT FURTHER EVALUATIVE ENQUIRY

METHOD 7.1   NOMINAL GROUP TECHNIQUE

This is a procedure that has some advantage over brainstorming reactions, in that the points generated are usually ranked. It has the following six stages:

1. question-setting;
2. reflection;
3. pooling;
4. clarification;
5. evaluation;
6. review.

The optimal size for a group is typically taken as about 10, with 15 as an upper limit. With larger numbers, split the group into two or more parallel activities, and then collate the outcomes.

> ## Example
>
> I attended a meeting recently at which the organizers took care to evaluate as the day progressed. In one such enquiry, we were asked what we were finding most useful (*question-setting*); we all had to jot down our response to that by ourselves (*reflection*). The facilitator then asked for examples, which she put up on a flip-chart, in full view (*pooling*). Once she had them, she doubled back to clarify what they involved (*clarification*).

We were then all given five votes – to be used as we thought fit. We came out and added our votes to the items on the list, but *not* as 'five-bar gates' of votes. We could give 3 to one item, 2 to another and none to anything else, of course. But in that case we had to write a '3' and a '2' as appropriate (*evaluation*).

In the open discussion of our priorities which followed we decided together to change the balance of the programme for the day (*review*); and we had the feeling that everyone, including those who had organized the programme, felt pleased that this was so.

In a similar, but somewhat lengthier, activity, a colleague asked students who were at the halfway stage in a student-centred module, what should be the priorities for the remainder of the group activities that formed a part of the module. This produced a list in which the weighting of activities and outcomes was markedly different from what the course team had planned.

It is important to note that the focus of this method is powerfully influenced by the choice and asking of the opening question. We have found it helpful with students who appreciate what formative evaluation can be and why it is important simply to ask 'What should be our immediate priorities for formative evaluation?' In that case, the method lives up to the promise of the chapter heading for this group of methods.

The immediate outcome of this particular example of enquiry was that the balance of the programme concerned was significantly changed. The longer-term impact of the feedback was that those who had planned the event or programme felt impelled to go back, and reconsider their processes, and ask themselves why these processes had not produced a programme which their participants or students would feel was adequate. The answers to those questions were not immediately apparent, and so the consequence was formative evaluation of the design process, as well as of the design outcome.

Notice in this, as in many other examples of formative evaluation, that the methods tend to be as powerful in shaping and reshaping teaching and learning activities *at the time* as in suggesting ways to make improvements for next time.

METHOD 7.2   Q-METHODOLOGY

This is regarded as a particularly important methodological tool for feminist research. It relies on the axiom that researchers should report, in an entirely non-judgemental form, the ways that women and men construct reality. It is particularly useful in situations where differences are likely to be important.

Data are gathered in a participant-centred way by means of a technique known as the Q-sort. Items are collected to represent the widest possible range of attitudes, opinions, beliefs and experiences on the topic to be studied. The subjects in the enquiry read each item in turn, and position it on a continuum according to its accuracy in representing their views. This has been compared with an R-type analysis by Senn.[1]

This approach, perhaps more a research methodology than a method for formative evaluation, is a specialist subject in itself, and merits detailed study. For that reason we will not attempt a brief summary here, but commend the publications as a stimulus to your thinking about yet another perspective.

OTHER METHODS THAT CAN POINT TO FURTHER ENQUIRY

In many cases the data produced by an enquiry is puzzling, and will call for further and more focused investigation. Almost all of the methods described so far could have such an outcome.

However, it is possible, in accordance with the two- (or more) stage approach to evaluation which has already been mentioned,[2] to set out deliberately to discover if there are aspects of the curriculum or of the learning experience which have hitherto gone without scrutiny, and which it might be profitable to make the subject of formative evaluation. For example:

Method 3.2   Dynamic lists of questions – can identify needs whose resolution should be investigated in detail, perhaps using recorded protocols.

Method 3.3   Observations – can often record behaviour which is not understood, or about which there is conjecture, and which thus is worthy of further and more detailed investigation.

Method 3.4   Critical incident technique – may identify aspects of the teaching and learning, the reasons for whose effectiveness or otherwise need to be ascertained.

Method 3.5   Talk-aloud protocols and Method 3.6   Journals, diaries and logs – may generate data which, having been provided by individuals, will often suggest possible findings whose generality it will be vital to check with a simple questionnaire approach, for example.

Method 3.7   Self-review – almost always leads to further evaluation as well as yielding information to aid curriculum development.

Several approaches can be directed specifically at the generation of topics that the students feel should be the subject of formative evaluation, or may generate these fortuitously. This would include: Method 3.8   Collecting comments from groups; Method 6.3   Delphi techniques; Method 6.5   A closing 'wash-up' session – perhaps with a preparatory session; and Method 6.8   Focus groups.

Some approaches will suggest topics for further and detailed evaluation when they generate surprise findings or evidence of what we have been calling 'mismatches' between student and teacher perceptions of what is happening, for example: Method 4.1   Identifying salient student constructs; Method 4.2   Interpersonal process recall; Method 4.3   Journals; Method 6.2   Interviews; Method 6.4   A letter to next year's students; and Methods 6.6–6.7   Rounds/Post-its.

Method 5.1   Concept mapping – will suggest the need for detailed study of learning when this is found to be generally incomplete, or, worse still, incorrect. Similar outcomes can emerge from Method 5.2   Pre- and post-testing and Method 5.3   Analysis of exam answers.

Method 6.1   Questionnaires – will often provoke further enquiries to find out why there are trends or discrepancies in students' reactions.

We often quote the contribution made by Wood,[3] a scientist, to a discussion of the abilities which are used in tertiary level studies and which may vary in importance from one discipline to another. Asked what was important, for example, in 'doing science' she thought for a little while and then suggested 'Noticing what is not there'.

This ability, of course, is the one that Sherlock Holmes found lacking in the faithful but seldom perceptive Dr Watson. You may recall that when Holmes was mulling over one particular case, he commented to Watson about the peculiar incident of the dog in the night-time. Watson, puzzled, pointed out that the dog had done nothing in the night-time – to which Holmes responded that this had, of course, been the peculiar incident.

We all need to be particularly alert in respect of noticing things which are not there in the coverage of our evaluations, and in seeking worthwhile suggestions about how these can be identified and included. That priority is what this chapter has been about – the identification of foci for the *next* formative evaluations.

Notes

1. Senn, C T (1996) Q-methodology as feminist methodology: women's views and experiences of pornography, in *Feminist Social Psychologies*, ed S Wilkinson, pp 201–17, Open University Press, Milton Keynes,.
2. See pp 27–28 above. This can often be a four-stage process: (1) macro-formative evaluation, which identifies major needs or possibilities for improvement; (2) micro-formative evaluation, which focuses on more detailed issues; (3) exploratory summative evaluation, which is answering 'what are the outcomes?'; (4) formal summative evaluation, which considers how *well* the outcomes have been achieved.
3. See Cowan, J (1998) *On Becoming an Innovative University Teacher*, Open University Press, Milton Keynes.

CHAPTER 8

Formative evaluation of assessment

WHY INCLUDE ASSESSMENT HERE, ANYWAY?

When we were thinking about the chapter titles – and the topics – for this book, we included in our first draft the notion of formative evaluation of assessment. This provoked surprised reactions. One of our colleagues commented that she had thought formative evaluation was 'really about teaching and learning and *that* bit of the education business'; and she queried if we could find anything useful to write, in any case, about the evaluation of assessment. We have the feeling that our colleague may not be the only one who would ask the question with which we open this chapter. And so we begin by attempting to provide a brief and persuasive answer.

It is our firm belief that the provision of assessment in our courses of higher education should be a top priority for formative evaluation because:

- it has been virtually disregarded up until now;
- it has a powerful effect (good or bad) on learning;
- all the evidence suggests that there is much scope and need for improvement.

We believe that the first of these points scarcely needs justification; we are not aware of any significant publication which addresses the purposeful evaluation and subsequent improvement of assessment in these terms.

Yet clearly assessment *does* have an influence, for better or for worse, on learning. We know, for example, that assessment can encourage surface rather than deep learning.[1] The hidden curriculum of assessment can establish priorities in terms of the learning outcomes towards which learners work,[2] which may well prove narrow and restricted. Surely anything, whether teaching or assessment, which has an influence on learning, should be evaluated, and should receive careful attention in our process of systematic development?

The evidence of the need for improvement is substantial, and frequently disregarded or unnoticed; consequently we find ourselves obliged to devote a separate section of this chapter to it.

THE NEED FOR IMPROVEMENT – AND HENCE FOR EVALUATION

Teaching practitioners in a number of disciplines[3] have long publicized the defects of our assessment systems in higher education, and many writers who are authorities in this field have made the case for review and improvement.[4] More recently, the framing of the remit to the assessors who undertake teaching quality assessment on behalf (initially) of the Higher Education Funding Council for England (and now the Quality Assurance Agency) has prompted a few intrepid assessors to examine the extent to which the chosen means and reality of assessment is compatible with the rhetoric of the declared vision, mission and aims of institutions and departments. Many important discrepancies and grounds for criticism have then emerged.

It is temptingly easier to offer and expand upon criticism than it is to suggest remedies. We have, therefore, set ourselves the obligation to offer in the section that follows a practical (and tested) response to each critical point that we will make in this present section. We are conscious that, for the sake of brevity and to avoid digressions, we are simply stating assertions. For our present purpose, we do not see that as a significant weakness; we are merely arguing that enquiries which will confirm or deny the validity of our assertions, at least in the particular cases with which formative evaluation should be concerned, are desirable.

Our view at the time of writing, then, is that:

1. It is common for assessors of teaching quality, who are charged to check practice against declared aims, to find that some institutional and course aims are clearly stated, yet nowhere covered in the assessment scheme.
2. It is the norm, rather than the exception, for internal and external academic auditors to be able to find module descriptors whose coverage is distinctly wider than that of the corresponding assessment scheme, and

review panels who are apparently blissfully unaware of this fact – or even that the possibility is worth checking.

3. That (often small) part of the syllabus in which candidates demonstrate a satisfactory grasp of the subject to gain a mere pass mark may well compare unfavourably with what is expected of a graduate in that discipline.

4. In project work, and elsewhere,[5] candidates frequently have erroneous impressions of the outcomes desired and the standards to which they should be working.

5. There are some reasonable grounds for fearing that candidates, especially in multiple-choice questions, have difficulty deciding what it is that the questions expect of them.

6. While assessment beyond Level 1 should focus on outcomes in which critical thinking plays a significant part, observations of candidates in examination rooms give few grounds for inferring that they devote much of their time there to such an activity.

7. Although examiners claim to know where borderlines lie within a range of marks, analyses of patterns of errors over that range often suggest that there is little difference in the *type* of errors made, but rather that the difference is located purely in the *frequency* of the error or weakness.

8. Few course reviews of which the writers have had sight of provide an analysis of the common errors to be found in the examination scripts or submitted work; yet these may be a sound and helpful indication of weaknesses in teaching or difficulties in learning.

9. Examiners and review boards have little access to data about students' reactions to examination or assignment tasks, and about how these tasks are undertaken.

10. Few course reviews investigate the reliability of assessment; and few examiners are familiar with the literature on this serious topic, and its recommendations.[6]

11. Assessed learning is significantly different from retained learning, and few course teams take steps to make themselves aware of the latter, or its implications.

HOW CAN THESE FACTORS BE EVALUATED?

We now offer you only suggestions that have been used in an ordinary department, by one (or more) serving university teacher(s). We do *not*, however, suggest that any department, or individual, should attempt all of our suggestions in one academic year, or for one subject or cohort of assessed students.

Since several of the suggestions which follow are simply variants on what has already been suggested for the formative evaluation of teaching and learning activities, the outlines which we give here are somewhat briefer.

We begin in each case with a direct and, we suggest, relevant question arising from the concerns we have just listed, and numbered accordingly. In offering our closing comments on the relevance of each question we are drawing on the first-hand experience of at least one of us.

Question 1   Is the assessed syllabus the same as the declared one?

You can check the extent of the agreement (or disagreement) between the declared and the assessed curricula, without undue attempts to produce quantitative results, in this way:

(a) List the aims and objectives that should be relevant to the course/ subject/module in question.

(b) Go through the assessment which the student must take, and inform yourself sufficiently to form your own judgement of the level of demand. What may appear to be critical thinking or thoughtful analysis, for example, could well be no more than regurgitation.

(c) Categorize assessment demands, and weightings, against the declared aims and objectives.

(d) Focus discussion on the more demanding or worthwhile aims and objectives, and consider the extent to which the assessment scheme covers them.

In the experience of one of us as a (TQA) assessor and academic auditor, a frequent finding has been the total absence of any demand in the assessed work for genuinely critical or original thinking listed in the aims.

Question 2   Does the assessment cover the listed learning outcomes?

We are concerned here with a more detailed scrutiny of, perhaps, a module with listed learning outcomes:

(a) List the outcomes in a matrix form.

(b) Analyse the assessment and, item by item, classify the coverage – with weights and due consideration of the implications of freedom of choice – against the outcomes.

(c) Look for, and expect, outcomes for which there is no assessment whatsoever, or for which assessment can be avoided through exercise of choice.

(d) Highlight omissions or possible evasions in coverage, and unduly light and heavy weightings which are seemingly worthy of consideration.

A typical finding in numerical subjects[7] has been a concentration on the use of familiar algorithms to tackle predictable worked examples, with no call for students to demonstrate deep understanding of the supposedly critical underlying concepts.

Question 3   In what parts of the assessed syllabus are candidates obtaining their marks?

(a) Seek a marking schedule, which may not be sufficiently detailed for your purposes. If so, obtain amplification of it from the marking examiners.

(b) Analyse all scripts for examinations or assignments to determine where the candidates actually scored their marks.

(c) Assemble this information in matrix form for consideration during the review process.

A typical finding in a subject answered in sentences and paragraphs has been the lack of displayed understanding in some of the more important parts of an assessed syllabus.

Question 4   Do the students know what is required of them?

(a) Ask the students, in small groups (probably snowballing for anonymity), to describe in their own words, and with weightings, the qualities or features of sound work in one or more assessed areas.

(b) Ask the examiners to do the same.

(c) Compare the descriptions prepared by students.

(d) Compare the students' descriptions with those by the staff.

(e) Arrange a non-threatening discussion by students and staff of these comparisons in the light of the question papers and students' scripts in the subject area in which the comparisons have been made.

Typical outcomes have included project students who had no concept of the desirability of thinking for themselves, and of questioning what they encounter and discover; and students who have answered essay questions in the firm belief that essay *style* was what mattered most, with content a little-mentioned second.

Question 5   Do the students understand the questions?

(a) Perhaps it is simplest to scrutinize this issue using last year's papers and assignments.

(b) Ask students to talk out their thoughts aloud or to a tape-recorder as they read a question, and think about how they would respond.

(c) Once they have done this – without attempting the questions or task – ask them to summarize what is *asked* of them.

(d) Ask the examiners to prepare a similar summary.

(e) Compare summaries, and report on similarities and discrepancies.

A typical outcome has been the shattering revelation that the demand of the question, as not unreasonably interpreted by the students, was quite different from what the examiner intended; and that the resultant poor performance by the student(s) could thus be no indication whatsoever of lack of learning.

Question 6　Can and do students think in examinations?

(a) Occupy part of the invigilators' time constructively. Ask them to count, from time to time and on their routine perambulations, how many students are producing work for the examination script – writing, calculating, looking up tables and so on, as the invigilator passes them; and how many are not.

(b) Plot the results against the time lapsed since the beginning of the examination. Then discuss these figures with the students, especially if you have data from several of their examinations to show them, and if this data describes or implies different behaviour.

(c) Ask if the detection of a high proportion of students who are active from the outset suggests lack of demand (or opportunity) to think; and if a low proportion later implies that the questions have all been answered, or that later questions present difficulties which need thought.

A typical outcome was summed up in the heartfelt quote from one (final year honours) student: 'Thinking is a luxury I cannot afford in these examinations'.

Question 7　Are there real differences in quality across the range of performances?

(a) Decide, perhaps iteratively, on roughly three categories of weaknesses that lose marks, and three that gain marks. In one such exercise, for example, one of us chose ignorance, serious errors and careless slips for the three types of weakness; and pertinent comment, succinct summarizing and use of relevant non-course material as the three types of strength.

(b) Take each script or assignment in turn, and classify where marks came – and went – according to these rough categories.

(c) Lay out your findings in ranking order of the total mark gained, down through the class.

(d) Take, perhaps, groupings of three students to iron out extreme individual differences; and sum up how each trio gained and lost marks according to the frequency with which different types of error were made, and different strengths displayed.

(e) Now describe the change in pattern as you go down through the list, trio by trio.

A typical outcome was the sad absence, in any great number, of strong points in the category that mattered most to the examiner, even in respect of the highest achieving students. Another was the surprising discovery that poorer candidates in a certain subject simply made *more* mistakes and offered *fewer* strong points without any change in the relative proportions of the points in the various performances or their individual worth, as determined by the markers.

Question 8 What does the assessed work suggest about the presence of common weaknesses?

(a) Review the assessed work.

(b) Tabulate the frequency of occurrence of common mistakes or weaknesses.

(c) Arrange for a detached consideration by students and assessors of the reasons that these have arisen, and the action that can or should be taken.

(d) Consider all possibilities, including ineffective teaching, a difficult topic for all students at all times, an inappropriate assessment item, or factors associated with the timing of the learning or last-minute revision (which may have been in competition, perhaps, with the World Cup).

A typical outcome was the discovery of a totally different pattern of weaknesses in one question in the same Open University exam for the two groups of students in one city who had been taught by different tutors. Another was the identification of an underlying weakness in handling sign conventions which, when made the subject of special remedial teaching, led to an appreciable improvement in performance on the part of subsequent cohorts.

Question 9   Do examiners know how students react to their questions and tasks?

To some extent, the best way we know to obtain an answer to this question is somewhat of an extension to the method suggested for Question 5:

(a) Promise three or four students anonymity if they will help you by going through their reactions to a recent assignment.

(b) After the marking has been completed, but before the final marks are declared, ask them to talk out their thoughts aloud to an enquirer (*not* you), or to a tape-recorder, as they recall reading a question, and as they then rethink how they decided to respond.

(c) Get them to go on, and begin to prepare their response (again).

(d) Once they have done this – without actually attempting the questions or task – ask them to summarize what was asked of them, and how they set out to tackle that.

(e) Summarize what the three or four subjects have told the enquirer without in any way suggesting that these findings are typical. Bring out similarities and differences between responses.

(f) Use this summary to ask other students, anonymously, how *they* recall that they responded and reacted.

(g) Inform the examiners accordingly.

A typical outcome was the unwelcome discovery that the majority of students prepared their response by asking themselves what their teacher would want them to include, opine and write. Another was the revelation that the majority of students in one class group depended on memory, rather than understanding, of points which would have emerged easily had they been able to rely upon understanding.

Question 10 How reliable is the marking process?

It is the common ignorance among academics of what is already known about lack of reliability and its causes, and the ineptness of the allegedly adequate (and often costly) procedures which are adopted to overcome the risk of unreliability, which makes this question perhaps the most important in our list.

We would strongly advise that, regularly:

(a) Briefed examiners, including examiners of project work, should agree a marking schedule, and then *blind* and *anonymously* double-mark all work in one set which bears no annotations from the first examiner.

(b) The same examiners, or a subset of them, should remark at some later date, in the same way.

(c) The reliability of the consequent marking should be analysed statistically by someone competent to do so, and the implications, in terms of revised decisions, should be made explicit.

(d) There should be discussion of the cases in which the discrepancies are large – *not* to resolve the difference, but to identify the possible causes of such a difference.

(e) The examination board should devise or revise its own procedures and requirements consequently; but, in addition, individuals may wish to work with heightened awareness of the particular occasions when their marking may profit from a second or third opinion.

(f) Reference should then be made to the literature on inter-*examination* reliability,[8] which is an even greater concern than the inter-*examiner* reliability figuring in this set of enquiries.

A typical outcome was the discovery that gross discrepancies *did* occur on occasion, that they were associated with what might reasonably be described as a 'bee in the bonnet' of one examiner, and that once that particular 'bee' had been identified and acknowledged the examiner knew when to worry about the reliability of marking on a future occasion.

Another typical outcome was the shock occasioned when, practice having led to apparently reliable double (but not blind) marking with fairly consistent results, the arrangement described above revealed horrifying inconsistencies in a few, but an important few, cases – once the annotations of the first marker were not available to the second marker.

Question 11   Does the assessment confirm that enduring learning has taken place?

This is a question that is important, for example, when prerequisites and their assessment are being considered, or when the effectiveness of the teaching and learning situations are under review. It is or should be also especially important in the case of examinations that earn recognition from a professional body.

You could proceed in this way:

(a) Take an examination paper from, say, June in a particular year.

(b) Without warning, administer it to a continuing class in the same subject in the November. Make it clear that performance, since it confirms prerequisite learning, is and will be important. (You don't need to tell them just yet that while it *is* important, it will not count in the assessment of the course/module on which they are now engaged. Nor, of course, should you imply an untruth.)

(c) Mark to the previous schedule and standards.

(d) Compare marks.

(e) Compare also where marks were gained – and lost.

A typical outcome has been a drop overall to 0.6 of the June score with some students scoring 0.1 of the June score, and others 1.6 times the June score. More significantly, a typical outcome has been apparent lack of comprehension (in June and – more importantly – in November) of certain concepts from the previous module on which teaching and learning in the current module were asserted to depend.

Should we have formative evaluation of assessment, then?

At the beginning of this chapter, we outlined three reasons, which seemed to us to be sound, for engaging in formative evaluation of assessment.

In conclusion, we approach this question rather differently – from consideration of the potential outcomes, and the ease with which they can be obtained. We would always want to put heavy stress on formative evaluation of assessment in routine programme reviews because:

- it is often the most immediate and important source of information about weaknesses in the course which require attention;
- it relates directly and (presumably) somewhat objectively to the learning with which we, and the students, are engaged;
- its findings are usually quite persuasive, even to the cynics.

Notes

1. Ramsden, P (1992) *Learning to Teach in Higher Education*, Routledge, London; Marton, F and Säljö, R (1976) On qualitative differences in learning: outcome and process, *British Journal of Educational Psychology*, **46**, pp 4–11.
2. See Snyder, B R (1971) *The Hidden Curriculum*, MIT, Cambridge, MA; Ramsden, P (1988) Studying learning: improving teaching, in *Improving Learning: New Perspectives*, ed P Ramsden, pp 13–31, Kogan Page, London.
3. eg Hill, B J (1972) An investigation into the consistency of marking examination scripts in BSc Pt I in Mechanical Engineering, *Higher Education*, **1** (2), pp 221–27; (1975) Reliability of marking in BSc examinations in engineering, *International Journal of Mechanical Engineering Education*, **3** (2), pp 97–106; McVey, P J (1972) The reliability of examinations in electrical engineering, *Report TR 24*, University of Surrey; Cox, R (1967) Examinations and higher education, *University Quarterly*, **21** (4), pp 292–340.
4. Rowntree, D (1977) *Assessing Students: How shall we know them?* Harper and Row, London; Heywood, J (1989) *Assessment in Higher Education*, 2nd edn, Wiley, Chichester.
5. See Cowan, J (1998) *On Becoming an Innovative University Teacher*, Open University Press, Milton Keynes.
6. See Heywood, quoted in Note 4 above.
7. Brohn, D M and Cowan, J (1977) Teaching towards an understanding of structural behaviour, *The Structural Engineer*, **55** (1), pp 9–17.
8. See, for example, McVey, quoted in Note 3 above.

CHAPTER 9

ACTION RESEARCH AND ITS IMPACT ON STUDENT LEARNING

The context of this book has been the development of what is regarded as the sound educational practice of engaging in a systematic process of curriculum development.[1] The element that has been claimed to make this process systematic is an informed progression from one iteration to the next, in which the evaluation of the present iteration informs and contributes to the next iteration.

Thus formative evaluation has come to be given the status it deserves in the process of curriculum development. Initially it amounted to little more than peer review, on a subjective basis, supplemented by the feedback from questionnaires which told teachers what students felt about the course experience they had just completed. Later, when an entirely new course was being conceived, it was at least occasional practice for pilot projects to be set up to test the innovation rigorously before it was put into regular use. Evaluation was at this stage and for this purpose largely a specialist activity for professional education researchers. Inevitably the potential value of such evaluations was limited by the fact that individual innovations on their own were a difficult source from which to extract the generalizable and nomothetic findings for which educational researchers yearn.

Consequently, and at first almost apologetically, some teachers who aspired to improve their teaching through better understanding of the nature of the interactions between themselves and their students, began to engage in ideographic enquiries. They fully recognized that these studies would produce findings which related only to themselves, teaching *their* subject to *their* students in *their* way and in *their* situation. But they deemed such outcomes relevant, informative and above all of direct use.

Gradually such activities led educationalists such as Cross and Angelo[2] to offer what those in the United States have called 'classroom assessment techniques', and what have been described by some in the UK as 'tools of enquiry'[3] for formative evaluation.

The choice of name for these techniques is not of great importance, though the transatlantic options may say something about the regard in which these educational communities hold formative evaluation of teaching. The point of interest in the present context is that teachers who wanted to action-research their own practices and processes, whatever the limitations of that activity, have now been offered and have begun to use purposeful methods to obtain reliable data on which their self-evaluations and consequent further development could be based. Moreover, there has been a growing appreciation of the value of qualitative as well as quantitative data, and so phenomenological and illuminative studies[4] have become increasingly common and acceptable.

It is our oft-repeated argument in this book that formative evaluation is an essential element in curriculum development. We would also suggest that a development of formative evaluation, in the form of action research, is an essential strategy for the teachers who wish to construct a truly professional basis for their own development of practice and expertise. Moreover, we maintain that this strategy is one whereby teachers can develop the kind of relationship with their students which offers an appropriate context for the development of their skills and their awareness of the process of learning which is now increasingly an explicit part of any curriculum.

Teachers who have regularly engaged in action research into their own teaching have found, in our experience, that this practice has given them insight into the nature of their students' learning which has enabled them to make marked changes to their teaching in style and emphasis, and in their approach to student individuality, leading to statistically significant improvements in students' learning. The approach has given them the rigorous and sound basis upon which to construct a truly professional habit of reflection-on-action-in-action.

However, we would wish to take the use of tools of formative enquiry one stage further – into the arena of student learning – as a tool for *their* development as reflective learners. We would draw a parallel between what has proved useful and effective for *teachers* in facilitating improvement in *their* process and practice in teaching, and what should and can prove effective for *learners*, in facilitating improvement in the cognitive and interpersonal processes and practices which increasingly feature on *their* learning agendas.

Three examples will, we hope, illustrate what we mean by the possibilities of this approach. In the first, one of us, using the method of recorded protocols, found that the workload was simply too much for the secretarial support available to him. So he resolved to get his students to analyse their own protocols, and to check the findings with other students. Rapidly the students became researchers and developers of their own practice, leading the teacher to realize that it really mattered little that *he* knew how his students solved problems; for what really mattered and would prove productive was what that *they* knew how they solved problems, and that they pondered constructively on that information. So he progressed to the design and provision of learning activities in which students were encouraged to develop process abilities, such as problem-solving, through researching their own practices and processes. As a result, these students who had developed the ability to be aware of their cognitive processes, whatever their level of ability in conventional classes, moved up the ranking order in subjects which they were not taught by the tutors who concentrated on process awareness.[5]

The other one of us experienced as a student the power of the habit of self-assessment in the curriculum at Alverno College. She undertook, as a new student, the initial diagnostic tests on basic skills where the session afterwards with the assessor focuses, not on how well you have *done*, but on how well you have *judged* your performance. That emphasis on reflection and self-assessment is a key element of the competence-based curriculum at the college. From the very start, students build up the habit of being aware of the processes of their learning, of what is happening for them, and of judging rigorously their strengths and weaknesses at any stage. This has a dynamic impact on the nature of their learning. It gives them a real responsibility for their own learning, for they are the custodians of their own standards. They are not dependent on someone else to tell them how well they are doing; they know themselves, and have that confidence. By the fourth year, the role of the teacher is largely reduced to being the learned resource on the topic of the class; the students themselves have largely taken over responsibility for their learning, for their reflection on their own development and for their decisions, individually or in groups, about how to make progress.

As a result of this experience, the ex-Alverno student finds that rigorous self-assessment is now a habit which pays off substantially in all aspects of her professional life. As a researcher and continuing learner, it gives her greater motivation and justified confidence. It enables her to be more directed and purposeful in her work; in one case, where she was recently moving into research in an unfamiliar historical period, it gave her the tools for analysis of process which enabled her to maximize her use of previous experience, and to target key areas for enquiry, formulating sharp and productive questions. In teaching and in management, likewise, the ability to identify the key points for development and the kind of support needed make for a satisfying continuum of development, rather than the reactive lurches of the past!

We have already mentioned our colleague who experimented with the use of Kelly's Repertory Grid to gain insight into her students' learning.[6] She has since sought ways to build in, as a matter of routine, the feedback from students to tutor about the nature of their reactions to, and preferences for, correspondence tuition. In doing so, she explained her purpose and findings to them, prompting them in turn to think about and improve the process which they followed when reading her comments, and reacting to them. Hence the learning process for these students deepened and became more effective and meaningful as their involvement in the process of self-enquiry prompted them, in turn, to think more carefully than ever before about their actions as they learned, and about how these could be improved.

More and more emphasis is being placed in education on the higher-level cognitive skills, such as analysis, problem-solving and the making of judgements; and on interpersonal abilities, which matter increasingly in professional and social life. We know that these abilities develop when learners are encouraged to reflect on process, analytically in the manner advocated by Kolb[7]; and when they do so evaluatively as well as analytically, following the approach described in Schön.[8] Such reflection should not be subjective, and self-sufficient: it will be more profitable if and when it is informed by data on which the learner can rely, and from which developmental reflection can result. We suggest that one way of encouraging the constructive thinking which we call metacognition about processes and practices[9] is to provide students with tools of enquiry that they can put to good use in fuelling such metacognition.

We are firmly convinced that there is the same potential waiting to be harnessed if practicable tools of enquiry are offered to *students*, as there has been realization of potential when practicable tools of enquiry have been made available to *teachers*. For example, we recall the improvement that Cowan[10] obtained in first-year project and small-group work by equipping students with such tools as the means of obtaining basic analyses of interpersonal behaviour. He enabled his students to use these tools to good effect, and to enhance the effectiveness of the groups in which they worked. Similarly we believe that any of the tools of enquiry, such as the dynamic list of questions, could equally well be used by students, though for a subtly different purpose from that of a teacher-user. Students can profit from improvement of their cognitive and interpersonal processes and practices. These should surely lie at the heart of their learning in any worthwhile degree nowadays, whatever the discipline area.

Thus it would be feasible for there to be more carefully planned teaching and learning situations in which teachers and students together, and with similar methodologies, will research their own processes, reflect upon them together and bring about improvements in both the teaching and the learning.[11]

Notes

1. For example, Davies, I K (1971) *The Management of Learning*, McGraw-Hill, Maidenhead; Romiszowski, A J (1981) *Designing Instructional Systems: Decision making in course planning and curriculum design*, Kogan Page, London, and many others.
2. Angelo, T A and Cross, K P (1993) *Classroom Assessment Techniques*, 2nd edn, Jossey-Bass, San Francisco.
3. For example, Cowan, J and George, J W (1997) *Formative evaluation, bordering on action research*, (Project Report 97/5), Open University in Scotland, Edinburgh; Hewitt, P *et al* (1997) *How do I know I am doing a good job?*, Open University, Open Teaching Toolkit, Edinburgh.
4. See Parlett, M and Hamilton, D (1972) *Evaluation as illumination: a new approach to the study of innovatory programmes*, University of Edinburgh, Centre for Research in Educational Sciences; Robson, C (1993) *Real World Research: A resource for social scientists and practitioner-researchers*, pp 303–04, Blackwell, Oxford.
5. Cowan, J (1986) *Education for Capability in Engineering Education*, D.Eng thesis, Heriot-Watt University, Edinburgh.
6. See Method 4.1, pages 57 and 121.
7. Kolb, D A (1984) *Experiential Learning*, Prentice Hall, New York.
8. Schön, D A (1983) *The Reflective Practitioner*, Basic Books, New York; (1987) *Educating the Reflective Practitioner*, Jossey-Bass, London; (1991) *The Reflective Turn*, Teachers College Press, New York.
9. Biggs, J B (1985) The role of metacognition in enhancing learning skills, *Proceedings of the Annual Conference of the Australian Association for Research in Higher Education*, Hobart.
10. See Cowan, J, *Education for Capability in Engineering Education*, D.Eng. thesis, Heriot-Watt University, Edinburgh.
11. Cowan, J (1995) Research into student learning – yes, but by whom?, in *Teaching Science for Technology at Tertiary Level*, ed S Törnkvist, Royal Swedish Academy of Engineering Sciences, Stockholm; Geddes, C and Wood, H M (1995) *The evaluation of teaching transferable skills in science*, (Project Report 95/1), Open University in Scotland, Edinburgh.

APPENDIX REMINDER SHEETS FOR COLLEAGUES WHO ASSIST YOU

While we hope the descriptions in this book have been adequate for your purposes, we are aware from our own experience that it is simpler to recruit a colleague to assist us if we can tell them exactly what we would like them to do. The following notes are intended to be available to you for that purpose – handouts that you can talk through with a colleague assistant, and pass on to them as a reminder of what they are to do 'on the day'. We have picked out only those methods where that task is not one that will be immediately clear, and where the colleague will be more helpful to you if they can investigate as intended.

Method 3.2   Dynamic lists of questions

If the activity is to be evaluated in several parts, and if you wish to ascertain what each part contributes to the overall learning experience, you will probably benefit from asking a colleague to assist you. (In this approach it is still possible for you to handle all the technicalities and back up work yourself.)

Here is what that assisting colleague and the teacher should do in such a situation:

1. Before the activity begins, the teacher concerned will ask each student to make a private list of the questions (other than a problem sheet question) for which they hope to have obtained answers before the teaching activity concludes.

2. The teacher will promise that, if the student wishes, any outstanding questions will be dealt with, individually, at the end of the teaching activity. The teacher explains that the purpose of the exercise is to ensure that as many of the student needs as possible are resolved in the course of the activity.

3. The colleague collects the sheets, and photocopies them.

4. The sheets are returned as quickly and unobtrusively as possible at an appropriate break in the activity.

5. The teacher proceeds in the usual style.

6. The teacher reminds the students on occasions to keep an eye on the list of questions, deleting any which are answered as the activity proceeds, and adding any new ones that the tuition generates.

7. At the end of the first part, the students are asked to ensure that their question sheets are updated; answered questions are to be scored through, and any new questions which have arisen are to be added.

8. The colleague collects the sheets, and photocopies them carefully, keeping this bundle separate.

9. Steps 4–8 are repeated for each part into which the teacher has separated the activity.

10. At the end of the activity, the teacher offers each student the opportunity to ask the unanswered questions, and does all that is possible to deal with them, to the students' satisfaction, before the class closes.

11. The teacher asks the students to update the sheets, as in step 7, for the last time.

12. The assistant summarizes the data initial needs, needs discovered during the activity and unresolved needs – all of which should be qualified with an indication of the frequency with which these occur in the class group.

13. The declaration of unanswered questions informs the teacher about expectations that the students had of the activity, and which were not fulfilled until the end.

14. If the students are prepared to talk to the teacher about the entire list, that is further informative evaluation.

15. In all of the above, the use of pseudonyms and the involvement of the colleague in summarizing can reassure students to be as frank and accurate as possible.

Method 3.3   Observations

In some cases, the teacher will leave the assisting colleague to determine the focus and method of recording of observations, In such unbriefed observing, which may occur for the very good reason that the teacher is hoping for a different perspective – and does not wish to pre-empt that by briefing the observer on what to observe, or how to obtain data – we suggest a brief along these lines:

1. Find out the aims and objectives that the teacher is working to, and also find out, preferably from the students, what information they have about the intended learning outcomes for the activity you will observe.

2. Note any discrepancies – and in particular any vagueness on the part of the learners about what the activity is to be about.

3. Plan a way to observe and record observable evidence, if there is any, of what learning outcomes have, and have not (the latter probably easier) been achieved in the activity.

4. Ask the teacher for the lesson plan – before the event.

5. Check out this plan against the intended learning. Will the outcomes in mind be covered? Will the outcomes be approached in a manner appropriate to their level?

6. Plan to observe and record the reality of events in comparison with the teacher's intentions.

7. Predict the behaviour to be expected of students – whether note-taking, interaction in group work or participation in seminars. Think of the extremes of behaviour, from that which would give *you* great satisfaction as a teacher to that which would depress you utterly. These extremes should suggest to you aspects of behaviour that you can observe, record and usually count. For example, you could note the number of times students are still writing furiously when an overhead transparency is being removed from the projector; the number and nature of questions of clarification which are asked of the teacher (or of classmates) when a task is declared; or the frequency with which students in seminar groups talk directly to each other, and not to the teacher.

8. Plan appropriate observations. Consider the use of a pre-prepared checklist or schedule to aid your observations. This will focus your attention; it leads to quickly made records in an appropriate form, which can be readily and comparably summarized and analysed; it also lessens the burden of recording while events occur. But it depends on your being familiar with the checklist, and coping in addition with any

significant but unexpected events which it is difficult to accommodate in the checklist.

9. Subdivide your time and allocate it to a sequence of different types of observation, as now semi-decided; include in that planning short periods for scanning the class behaviour for signs of significant occurrences not covered by your plan. For example, you may notice gender differentiation in participation, or pertinent questioning and commenting by students, which suggests healthy learning and deep thought.

10. Keep a note of times during which you observe with one priority or another and when events happen.

11. Remember that you will have to have more than one point in mind as you observe. Your noting of the sequence of events, in relation to the plan, is something that should continue throughout the activity, for instance.

12. Always reserve your right to change your intentions radically if you see or find good reason for so doing. Any significant behaviour that attracts your attention may well call for you to concentrate upon that, rather than on your original focus.

13. Sum up your observations factually. Volunteer no opinions or judgements, and preferably try to avoid forming judgements other than those that are desirable to observe and record.

14. Once you have assimilated and summarized your data, you may, of course, if so requested, and if you wish, discuss your interpretation of it with your teaching.

Method 3.5   Talk-aloud protocols

In this method, which seeks to elicit student reactions to materials or situations in which the teacher or course team have a personal investment, it is almost essential to enlist detached assistance. At the same time, though, the enquirer will need to establish a relationship with the subjects in order to encourage ease of reporting and frankness. Notice that, if this is taken as the first stage in a two-stage process, it is not necessary to obtain a representative sample, and it is probably best to seek subjects who are likely to be readily articulate.

The method may be applied to any activity in which students work individually, and respond to materials or tasks, rather than to a person. The allocation of duties would be as follows:

1. The teacher should ask three students (or sets of three) to help in an evaluation.

2. The evaluator should meet the subjects, perhaps initially with the teacher, but then on their own. It is desirable to arrange something semi-social so that the students become comfortable with the stranger. A snack or meal, with a light drink, is one such way of breaking the ice, and of thanking the students for their co-operation (in advance!).

3. The evaluator must promise them that nothing they say or do will go back to the teacher attributed to them; the evaluation will simply report that 'one students said (or did)…'. And the evaluator should assure them that the last part of the exchange will be to check if there is any aspect of the findings which is not to be reported back.

4. The evaluator now asks one student to tackle the task – working at a PC on teaching and learning software, or trying to solve a problem on a worksheet, or using printed learning materials – whatever it is that you are evaluating.

5. The evaluator asks the subject to talk out their thoughts as they go along. It is probably best to begin the task yourself, talk out your thoughts, and ask the student to do 'something like that, but for your thoughts and feelings'. Make sure you include feelings: 'What a horrible colour – it puts me off' or 'I hate switching back and forward from mouse to keyboard'.

6. Suggest to the two other students that they should ask questions if they need to so that if the talker were to be called away to the telephone, one of the others could carry on in the same way as the talker would have done. Warn them not to enter into discussion.

7. Retire to the background, and make notes of what seem important points for the talkers.

8. After 15–20 minutes, let one of the others be the active student who does the talking.

9. Then after another 15–20 minutes, repeat the process.

10. Now summarize what has seemed important to you as you listened.

11. Mention differences and similarities. Let the learners tell you if you have got it right. Make corrections and additions.

12. Ask their permission to report back, with a certain degree of anonymity, of course, as you won't be saying which one it was when you report that 'One of them…'.

13. Now the enquirer compiles a list of statements that sum up the reactions and tactics of at least one of the students in the trio.

14. The teacher then issues copies of that to the class with a Likert scale from 'strongly agree' to 'strongly disagree', with a slot for 'doesn't apply to me' and asks for responses to declare the class experience.

15. The teacher then summarizes and analyses the returns.

Method 4.1 Identifying student constructs in relation to their learning

We list here the suggestions which we made recently to a colleague who was interested to discover how students in a class of about 40 react to the comments which he and his fellow tutors add to submitted written work. We suggested, and now suggest to you, that you ask a colleague to assist you in this way:

1. Wait until several sets of course work have been in for comment, so that the students and staff have become familiar with the subject being studied and with the teacher's style.

2. The teacher should explain to the students what they are going to do, and how the students can best help.

3. The enquirer should number the comments or responses that the teacher has added to the students' work.

4. The teacher should delay the return of the work and comments until the class group, or perhaps half of it, can meet.

5. The teacher returns the work so that the students can read the comments as nearly as possible according to their usual practice.

6. The enquirer now issues worksheets with a grid bearing numbers down the left-hand side up to the greatest number of comments provided. The enquirer asks each student to delete the numerals beyond the highest number on their own work.

7. The enquirer now introduces the notion of splitting trios into pairs and singletons. It is helpful to give the example of traffic-lights, a bus-stop and a lamp-post, and ask for private subdivision into a pair and a singleton, on the basis of some feature that is significant as far as street furniture is concerned. Point out that both lamp-post and bus-stop contain hyphens, and that the second word begins with the same letter as concludes the first word. But immediately point out that this is hardly a 'significant' feature of the two items, and would hardly tell us anything relevant about street furniture. Invite suggestions for meaningful subdivisions, and allow a little pondering time. Call for suggestions in plenary. Praise a division, for example, into two needing electricity (traffic-lights and lamp-post) and one not; or two stopping traffic (bus-stop and traffic-lights) and one not. Point out that the need for electric supply, and the effect on traffic are both significant features of street furniture.

8. Explain that we now move on to identify significant features of the comments which the teacher adds to written work. Have a copy of the grid on the overhead projector. Circle three numbers in column one. Ask each student to circle the same three numbers in column one, and then to

refer to these comments themselves on the hard copy, and – recalling their reaction – split the comments into a pair and a singleton.

9. Write a possible, but less likely, split factor at the top of the first column on your transparency – perhaps 'I didn't understand'. Ask each student to write their own splitting factors, which they will already have chosen, at the head of their column one.

10. Put ticks for the one or two comments which you describe as having *had* that factor; and a cross for the two or one which did *not*.

11. Now get the students to go through the other comments (indicating similarly on the transparency as if you were doing so, too) marking ticks for the factor being true of a comment, and a cross for not.

12. Circle on that first column three ticks, or three crosses; ask them to do the same on their proformas.

13. Repeat steps 8–11 with less direction for these three comments, and then for the entire list, in column two.

14. Now make a choice with, say, three which have ticks in column one, and crosses in column two, and then leave the students to go at their own pace, and complete the table until they can't split any more trios.

15. Circulate and assist any students at this stage who are having difficulty following this last instruction.

16. When they get to that stage, ask them if they can think of any other points about tutors' comments which matter to them which aren't at the heads of the columns. Get them to write these in, and carry out the tick/cross exercise once more.

17. Ask them to count the number of ticks for each heading, and note these totals beside the heading.

18. Ask them also to circle the type of comment which they most welcome and find most useful, and, if they so wish, to explain why, and finally to add their name to the form.

19. Collect the forms, and decide what they tell the teacher about the commenting, and how to comment in future.

Method 4.2   Interpersonal process recall

In this method, since you are one of the subjects as the involved teacher, you must have a colleague to help as the enquirer. This is what you should ask the enquirer to do:

1. Experience the method yourself, as a subject. Don't proceed with the enquiring task unless you find the experience exciting, and are prepared to share that enthusiasm with the students. The teacher should have done the same.

2. Find an early and informal opportunity to describe the process to the students who will be subjects to allay any concerns they may have. Share your genuine enthusiasm and wonder at the access to your memory that the process gave as you recruit and confirm volunteers to be subjects.

3. Make sure you have a quiet place with replay facilities ready for the unpacking session at the end of the tutorial.

4. Set up a video-camera aimed at the teacher in what will be as normal a teaching session as possible, and in a position which is as unobtrusive as possible. Make sure you are familiar with working the camera. Record either the entire session, or the agreed sections of it.

5. If you have recorded the entire session, select some 5–8 minutes of that recording covering a part of the teaching that interests either teacher or observer. Otherwise, use the tape of the agreed section.

6. Settle your student volunteer, and then replay the tape, stopping it when the subject's eyes or face suggest recall, or when the student calls 'Stop'.

7. Each time ask the same, pre-declared question: 'Does that remind you of how you were thinking or feeling – *at the time*?'

8. You may then ask follow-up questions to clarify.

9. All the time make notes – as fully as possible, but without slowing down the responses and recall.

10. Repeat this procedure with the teacher, again making notes.

11. Report to the teacher, and possibly also to the student if that is not awkward for the student, what has been elicited and the mismatches between the two perceptions.

12. Leave it to the teacher to check out the mismatches with other students, and then decide what to do.

REFERENCES

Angelo, T A and Cross, K P (1993) *Classroom Assessment Techniques*, 2nd edn, Jossey-Bass, San Francisco

Basch, C E (1987) Focus group interview: an under-utilised research technique for improving theory and practice in health education, *Health Education Quarterly*, **14**, pp 411–48

Belenky, M F *et al* (1986) *Women's Ways of Knowing: The development of self, voice and mind*, Basic Books, New York

Biggs, J B (1985) The role of metacognition in enhancing learning skills, *Proceedings of the Annual Conference of the Australian Association for Research in Higher Education*, Hobart, Australia

Boyd, H R, Adeyemi-Bero, A and Blackhall, R F (1984) *Acquiring professional competence through learner-directed learning – an undergraduate perspective*, Occasional Paper No 7, Royal Society of Arts, London

Boyd, H R and Cowan, J (1986) The case for self-assessment based on recent studies of student learning, *Assessment and Evaluation in Higher Education*, **10** (3), pp 225–35

Brohn, D M and Cowan, J (1977) Teaching towards an understanding of structural behaviour, *The Structural Engineer*, **55** (1), pp 9–17

Calder, J (1994) *Programme Evaluation and Quality*, Kogan Page, London

Chambers, E (1992) Improving foundation level study at the Open University through evaluation of the student experience, in *Proceedings of the CNAA Conference on 'Evaluating the quality of the student experience'*, London

Chodorov, N J (1996) Seventies questions for thirties women; Some nineties reflections, in *Feminist Social Psychologies*, ed S Williams, Open University Press, Milton Keynes

Cowan, J (1972) Is freedom of choice in examinations such an advantage?, *Technical Journal*, **10** (1), pp 31–32

Cowan, J (1977) Individual approaches to problem solving, in *Aspects of Educational Technology*, vol X, Kogan Page, London

Cowan, J (1980) Improving the recorded protocol, *Programmed Learning and Educational Technology*, **17** (3), pp 160–63

Cowan, J (1984) *Learning contract design: a lecturers' perspective*, Occasional Paper No 7, Royal Society of Arts, London

Cowan, J (1986) *Education for Capability in Engineering Education*, D.Eng thesis, Heriot-Watt University, Edinburgh

Cowan, J (1994) *Telephone interpersonal process recall*, Project Report 94/1, Open University in Scotland, Edinburgh

Cowan, J (1995) Research into student learning – yes, but by whom?, in *Teaching Science for Technology at Tertiary Level*, ed S Törnkvist, Royal Swedish Academy of Engineering Sciences, Stockholm, Sweden

Cowan, J (1998) *On Becoming an Innovative University Teacher*, Open University Press, Milton Keynes

Cowan, J and George, J W (1997) *Formative evaluation, bordering on action research*, Project Report 97/5, Open University in Scotland, Edinburgh

Cowan, J and Harding, A G (1986) A logical model for curriculum development, *British Journal of Educational Technology*, **2** (17), pp 103–09

Cowan, J *et al* (1988) *Report on project to assess tools for formative evaluation*, Open University in Scotland, Edinburgh

Cowan, J, Morton, J and Bolton, A (1973) An experimental learning unit for structural engineering studies, *The Structural Engineer*, **51** (9), pp 337–40

Cox, R (1967) Examinations and higher education, *University Quarterly*, **21** (4), pp 292–340

Davies, I K (1971) *The Management of Learning*, McGraw-Hill, London

Flanaghan, J C (1954) The critical incident technique, *Psychological Bulletin*, **15** (4), pp 327–58

French, T (1992) *Data for evaluation tapping significant experience – an approach to the critical incident technique*, Proceedings of the CNAA Conference on Evaluating the Quality of the Student Experience, Council for National Academic Awards, London

Further Education Unit (1991) *Towards an educational audit*, FEU, London

Garry, A M and Cowan, J (1987) To each according to his needs, *Aspects of Educational Technology*, Vol XX, pp 333–37, Kogan Page, London

Geddes, C and Wood, H M (1995) *The evaluation of teaching transferable skills in science*, Project Report 95/1, Open University in Scotland, Edinburgh

Gibbs, G (ed) (1995) *Improving student learning through assessment and evaluation*, Oxford Centre for Staff Development, Oxford

Gibbs, G (forthcoming) *Course Design in Higher Education*, H852, Open University, Milton Keynes

Harvey, J (ed) (1998) *Evaluation Cookbook*, Learning Technology Dissemination Initiative, Heriot-Watt University, Edinburgh

Hewitt, P *et al* (1997) *How Do I Know I Am Doing a Good Job?*, Open Teaching Toolkit, Regional Academic Services, Open University, Milton Keynes

Heywood, J (1989) *Assessment in Higher Education*, 2nd edn, Wiley, Chichester

Hill, B J (1972) An investigation into the consistency of marking examination scripts in BSc Pt 1 in Mechanical Engineering, *Higher Education*, **1** (2), pp 221–27

Hill, B J (1975) Reliability of examinations in BSc examinations in engineering, *International Journal of Mechanical Engineering Education*, **3** (2), pp 97–106

Hounsell, D, McCullouch, M and Scott, M (eds) (1996) *The ASSHE Inventory*, Centre for Teaching, Learning and Assessment, University of Edinburgh, and Napier University

Hounsell, D, Tait, H and Day, K (1997) *Feedback on Courses and Programmes of Study: A handbook*, UCoSDA, Edinburgh

Kagan, N (1975) Influencing human interaction: eleven years with IPR, *The Canadian Counsellor*, **9** (2), pp 74–97

Kelly, G A (1995) The Psychology of Personal Constructs, Norton, New York

Kolb, D (1984) *Experiential Learning*, Prentice Hall, New York

Laurillard, D (1993) *Rethinking University Teaching*, Routledge, London

Lee, M (1997) *Telephone tuition project report*, Open University in Scotland, Edinburgh

Low, G (1995) 'Hallelujah, very': responding to 'very' in questionnaire items, *Evaluation and Research in Education*, **9** (1), pp 15–28

McVey, P J (1972) The reliability of examinations in electrical engineering, *Report TR 24*, University of Surrey, Guildford

Marton, F and Säljö, R (1976) On qualitative differences in learning: outcome and process, *British Journal of Educational Psychology*, **46**, pp 4–11

Mason, R (1995) Evaluating technology-based learning, in *Innovative adult learning with innovative technologies*, ed B Collis and G Davies, Elsevier Science B V, Amsterdam, New York, pp 191–99

Munn, P and Drever, E (1990) *Using Questionnaires in Small-scale Research*, Scottish Council for Research in Education, Edinburgh

Oakley, A (1981) Interviewing women; a contradiction in terms, in *Doing Feminist Research*, ed H Roberts, Routledge and Kegan Paul, London

Oppenheim, A N (1996) *Questionnaire Design and Attitude Measurement*, Heinemann, London

O'Shea, T (1992) Evaluating the educational experience of students, *Proceedings of the CNAA Conference on 'Evaluating the quality of the student experience'*, London

Page, C F (1974) *Student Evaluation of Teaching – The American experience*, Society for Research into Higher Education, London

Parlett, M and Hamilton, D (1972) *Evaluation as illumination: a new approach to the study of innovatory programmes*, Occasional Paper 9, Centre for Research in Educational Sciences, University of Edinburgh, Edinburgh

Perry, W (1970) *Forms of Intellectual and Ethical Development During the College Years: A scheme*, Holt, Rinehart and Winston, New York

Race, P and Brown, S (1998) Learning from student feedback, in *The Lecturer's Toolkit*, Kogan Page, London

Ramsden, P (1988) Studying learning: improving teaching, in *Improving Learning: New perspectives*, ed P Ramsden, pp 13–31, Kogan Page, London

Ramsden, P (1992) *Learning to Teach in Higher Education*, Routledge, London

Revil, D (1992) Student experience of higher education and the role of libraries, *Proceedings of the CNAA Conference on 'Evaluating the quality of the student experience'*, London

Robson, C (1993) *Real World Research: A resource for social scientists and practitioner-researchers*, Blackwell, Oxford

Rogers, C R (1967) *On Becoming a Person*, Constable, London

Romiszowski, A J (1981) *Designing Instructional Systems: Decision making in course planning and curriculum design*, Kogan Page, London

Rowntree, D (1977) *Assessing Students: How shall we know them?*, Harper and Row, London

Schön, D A (1983) *The Reflective Practitioner*, Basic Books, New York

Schön, D A (1991) *The Reflective Turn*, Teachers College Press, New York

Scriven, M (1973) Goal-free evaluation, in *School Evaluation: The politics and the process*, ed E R House, University of Berkeley, CA

Senn, C T (1996) Q-methodology as feminist methodology: women's views and experiences of pornography, in *Feminist Social Psychologies*, ed S Wilkinson, pp 201–07, Open University Press, Milton Keynes

Shields, S A and Crowley, J J (1997) Appropriating questionnaires and rating scales for a feminist psychology: a multi-method approach to gender and emotion, in *Feminist Social Psychologies*, ed S Williams, Open University Press, Milton Keynes

Snyder, B R (1971) *The Hidden Curriculum*, MIT Press, Cambridge, MA

Tessmer, M (1993) *Planning and Conducting Formation Evaluations: Improving the quality of education and training*, Kogan Page, London

Thorpe, M (1988) *Evaluating Open and Distance Learning*, Longman, Harlow

Tyler, R W (1949) *Basic Principles of Curriculum and Instruction*, University of Chicago Press, Chicago

Weedon, E M (1994) *An investigation into using self-administered Kelly analysis*, Project Report 94/5, Open University in Scotland, Edinburgh

Williams, N (ed) (1979) *An Introduction to Evaluation*, London Schools Council, London

FURTHER READING

Black, P and William, D (1998) Assessment and classroom learning, *Assessment in Education*, **5** (1), pp 7–75

Bloom, B, Hastings, J T and Madaus, G F (1971) *Handbook of Formative and Summative Evaluation*, McGraw-Hill, New York, Maidenhead

Breakwell, G and Milward, L (1995) *Basic Evaluation Methods*, BPS Books, Leicester

Harris, D and Bell, C (1994) *Evaluating and Assessing for Learning*, 2nd edn, Kogan Page, London

Hawkins, J and Honey, M (1990) Challenges of formative testing: conducted situated research in classrooms, *Technical Report* No 48, 1–5, Bank Street College, New York

Koon, J and Murray, H G (1995) Using multiple outcomes to validate students' ratings of overall teacher effectiveness, *Journal of Higher Education*, **66** (1), pp 61–81

Lowe, A, Thurston, W and Brown, S (1983) Clinical approach to formative evaluation, *Performance and Instruction*, **22** (5), pp 8–11

McAlpine, L (1987) The think-aloud protocol: a description of its use in the formative evaluation of learning materials, *Performance and Instruction*, **26** (8), pp 18–21

Markle, S M (1979) Evaluating instructional programmes: how much is enough?, *NSPI Journal*, February, pp 22–24

Milne, J and Heath, S (1997) *Evaluation Handbook for Successful CAL Courseware Development*, MERTaL, Aberdeen

Pratt, D D (1997) Reconceptualizing the evaluation of teaching in higher education, *The Journal of Higher Education*, **34** (1), pp 23–44

Ragan, S L and McMillan, J J (1989) The influence of student evaluative feedback on the improvement of clinical teaching, *The Journal of Higher Education*, **60** (6), pp 666–82

Rahilly, T (1991) Collecting feedback from learners: costs and benefits of different conditions, Paper presented to the annual meeting of the American Education Research Association, Chicago

Zuber-Skeritt, O (1992) *Action Research in Higher Education: Examples and reflections*, Kogan Page, London

Index

Note: Since this is a handbook, and not a textbook, we expect that many will want to find what they seek without re-reading, or even first-reading, the entire text. We want you to be able to find items that may be useful to you.

We have therefore provided a somewhat full 'users' index, within which there may well be some overlap and duplication. We have also indexed according to the spirit, rather than the letter, of the text. Thus 'reliability' includes 'reliable' and 'unreliable'; and 'recording, electronic' includes audio and video recording.